30 DAYS OF NIGHT
BEYOND BARROW

E OF ART

IDW Publishing • San Diego, CA

30 Days of Night: Beyond Barrow

story: steve niles

art: bill sienkiewicz

letters: robbie robbins & neil uyetake

edits: chris ryall

collection edits & design: dene nee

ISBN: 978-1-60010-155-7

11 10 09 08   1 2 3 4 5

IDW Publishing is
Ted Adams, President
Robbie Robbins, EVP/Sr. Graphic Artist
Chris Ryall, Publisher/Editor-in-Chief
Clifford Meth, EVP of
Strategies/Editorial
Alan Payne, VP of Sales
Neil Uyetake, Art Director
Tom Waltz, Editor
Andrew Steven Harris, Editor
Chris Mowry, Graphic Artist
Amauri Osorio, Graphic Artist
Dene Nee, Graphic Artist/Editor
Matthew Ruzicka, CPA, Controller
Alonzo Simon, Shipping Manager
Kris Oprisko, Editor/Foreign Lic. Rep

30 Days of Night created by
Steve Niles & Ben Templesmith

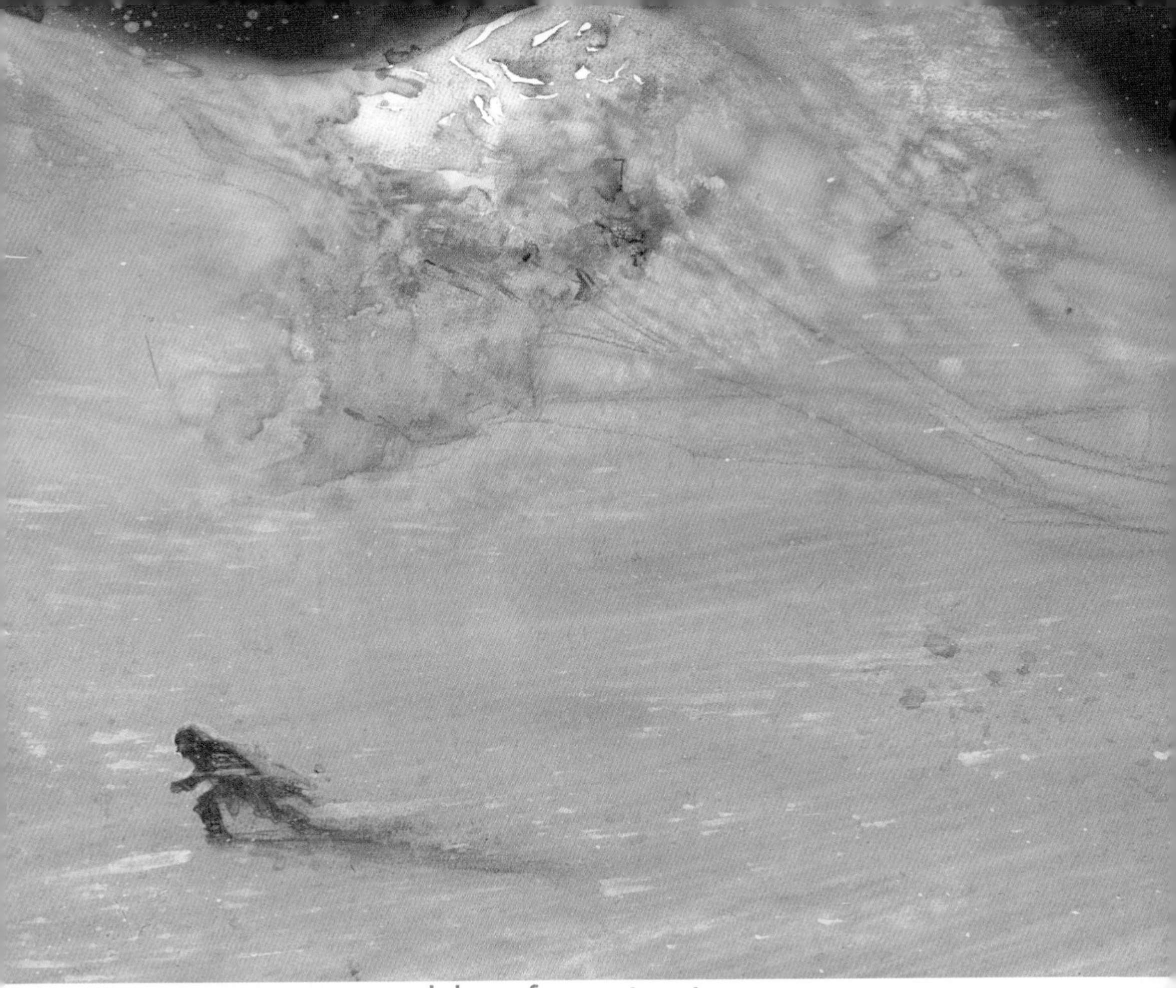

table of contents

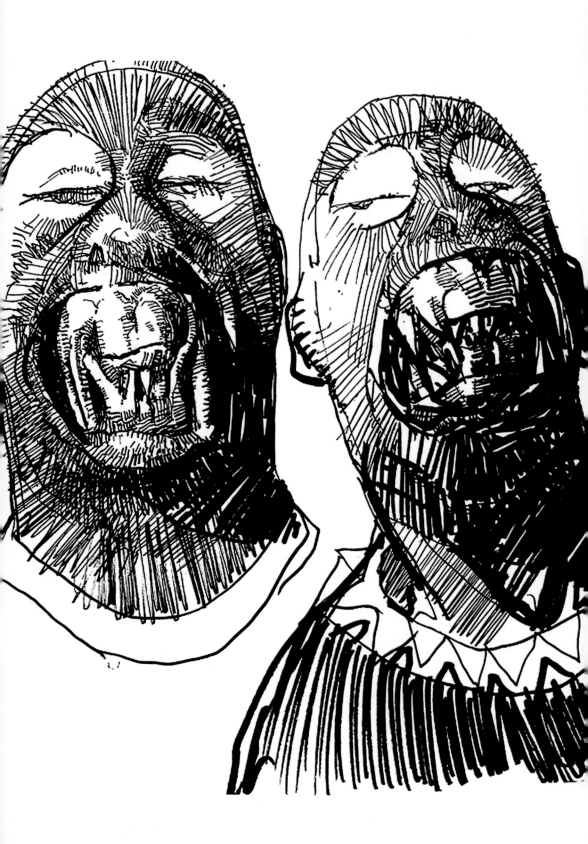

art by bill sienkiewicz

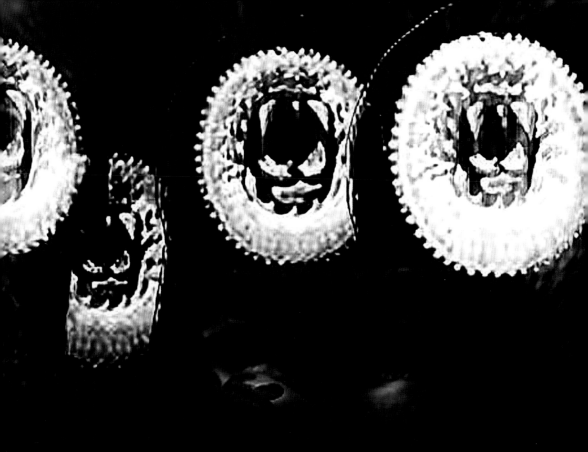

chapter one

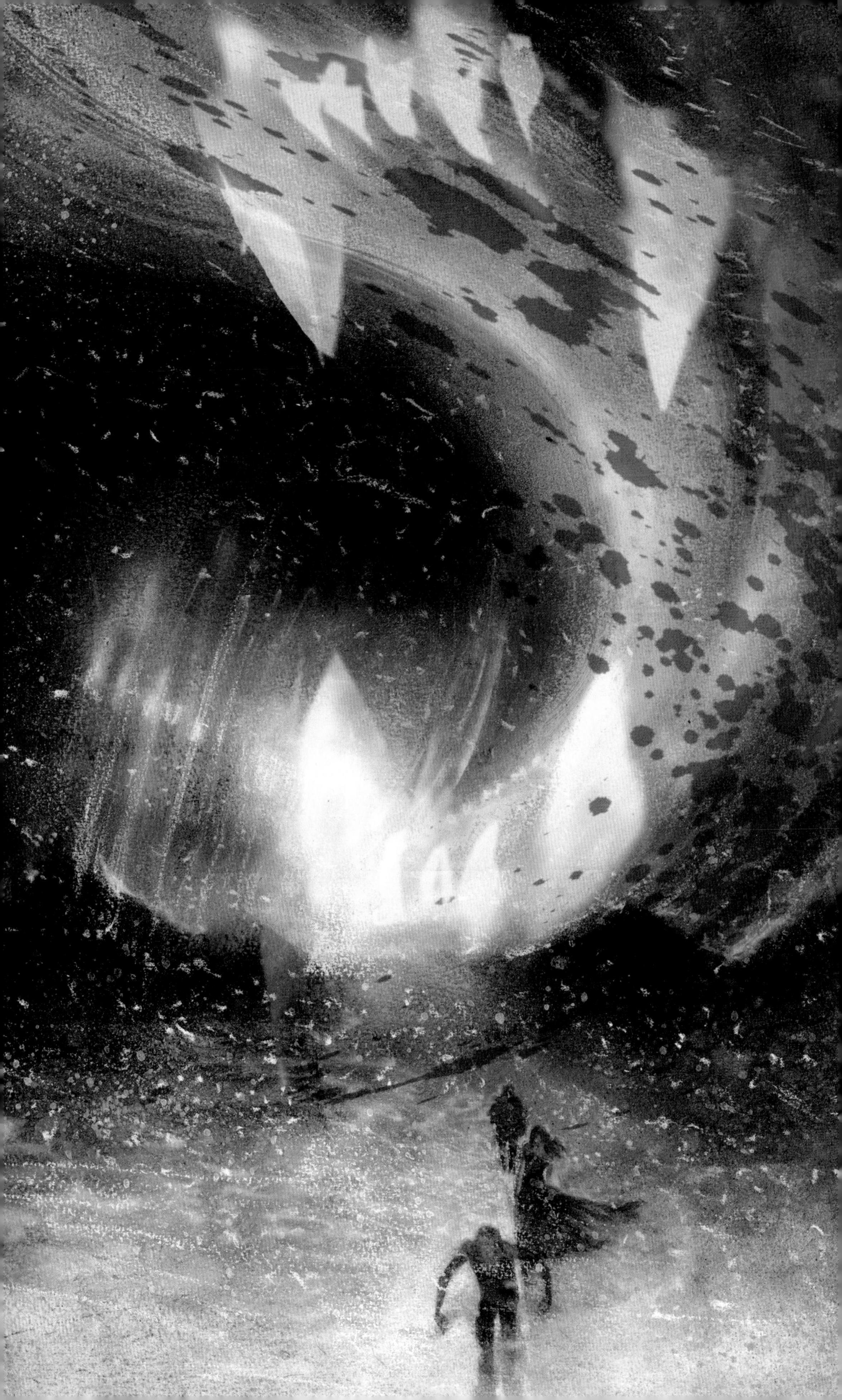

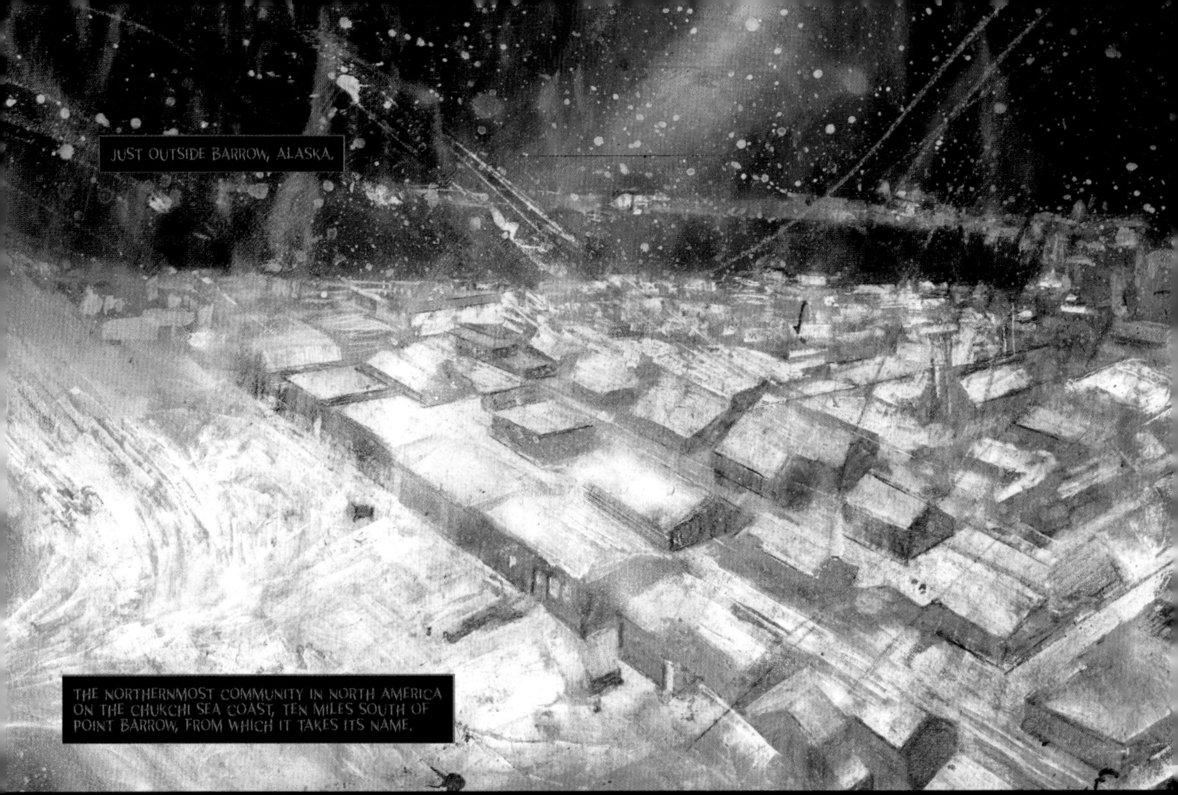
JUST OUTSIDE BARROW, ALASKA.
THE NORTHERNMOST COMMUNITY IN NORTH AMERICA ON THE CHUKCHI SEA COAST, TEN MILES SOUTH OF POINT BARROW, FROM WHICH IT TAKES ITS NAME.

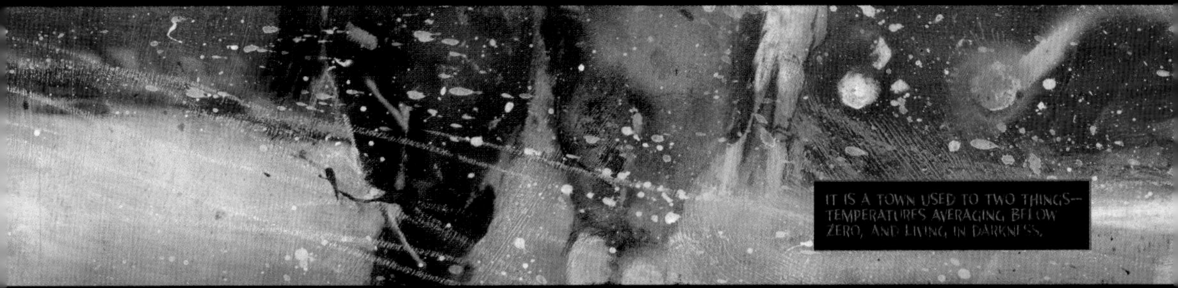
IT IS A TOWN USED TO TWO THINGS-- TEMPERATURES AVERAGING BELOW ZERO, AND LIVING IN DARKNESS.

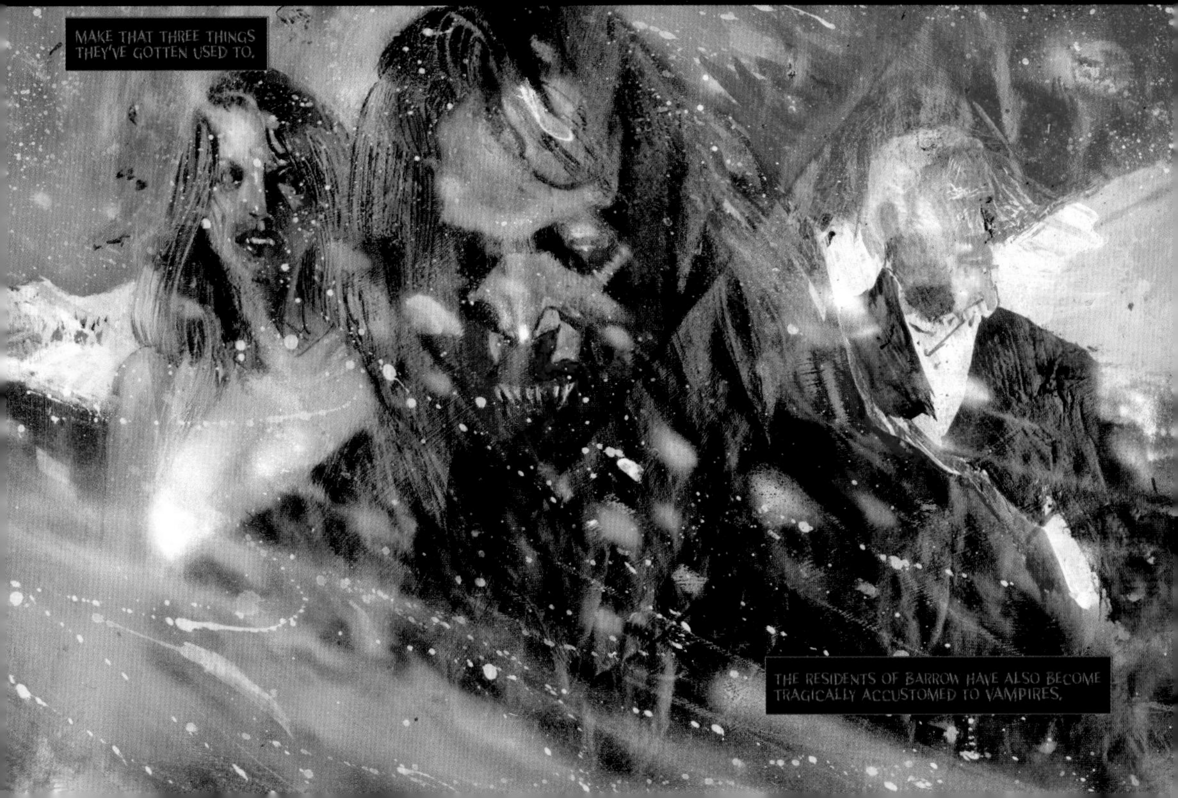
MAKE THAT THREE THINGS THEY'VE GOTTEN USED TO.
THE RESIDENTS OF BARROW HAVE ALSO BECOME TRAGICALLY ACCUSTOMED TO VAMPIRES.

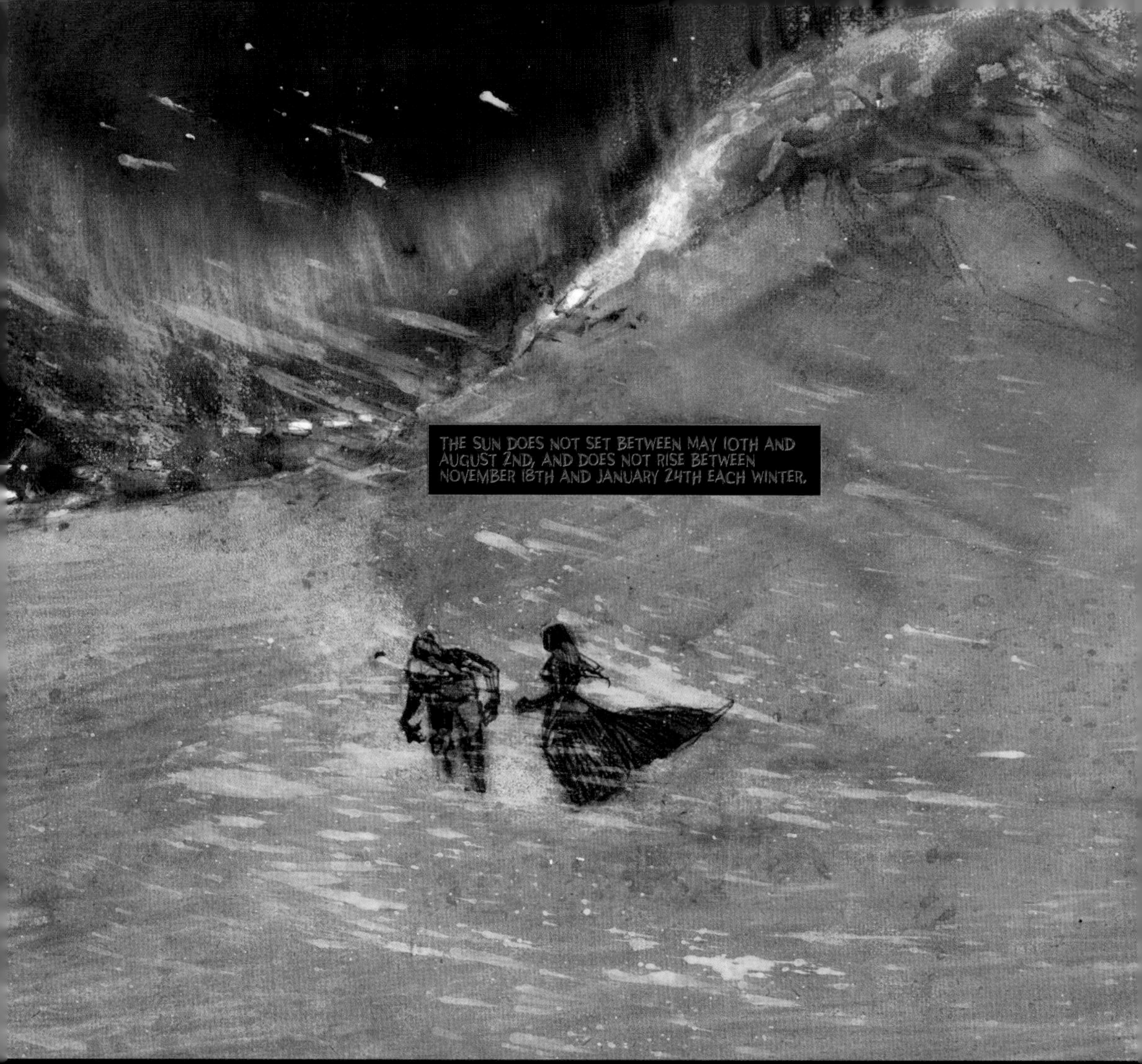
THE SUN DOES NOT SET BETWEEN MAY 10TH AND AUGUST 2ND, AND DOES NOT RISE BETWEEN NOVEMBER 18TH AND JANUARY 24TH EACH WINTER.
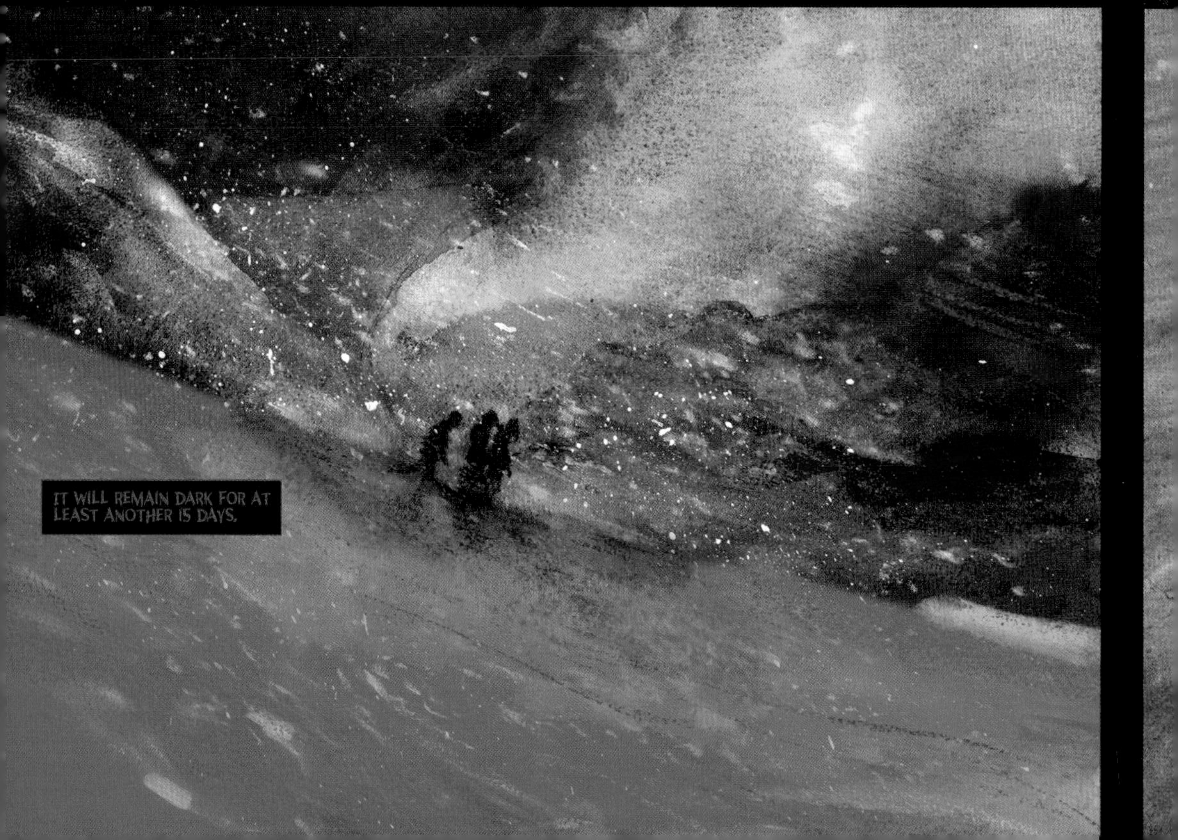
IT WILL REMAIN DARK FOR AT LEAST ANOTHER 15 DAYS.

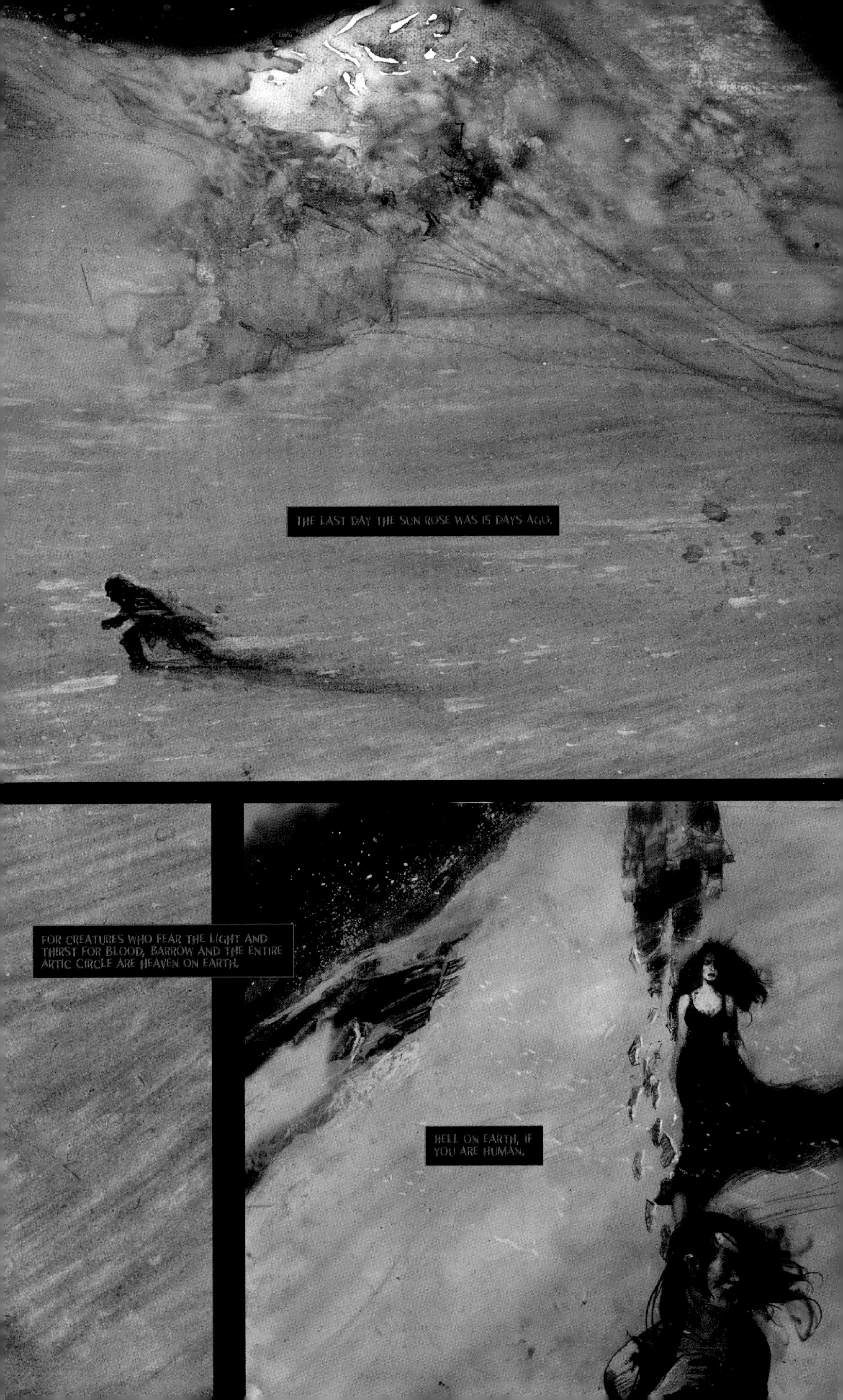
THE LAST DAY THE SUN ROSE WAS 15 DAYS AGO.
FOR CREATURES WHO FEAR THE LIGHT AND THIRST FOR BLOOD, BARROW AND THE ENTIRE ARTIC CIRCLE ARE HEAVEN ON EARTH.
HELL ON EARTH, IF YOU ARE HUMAN.

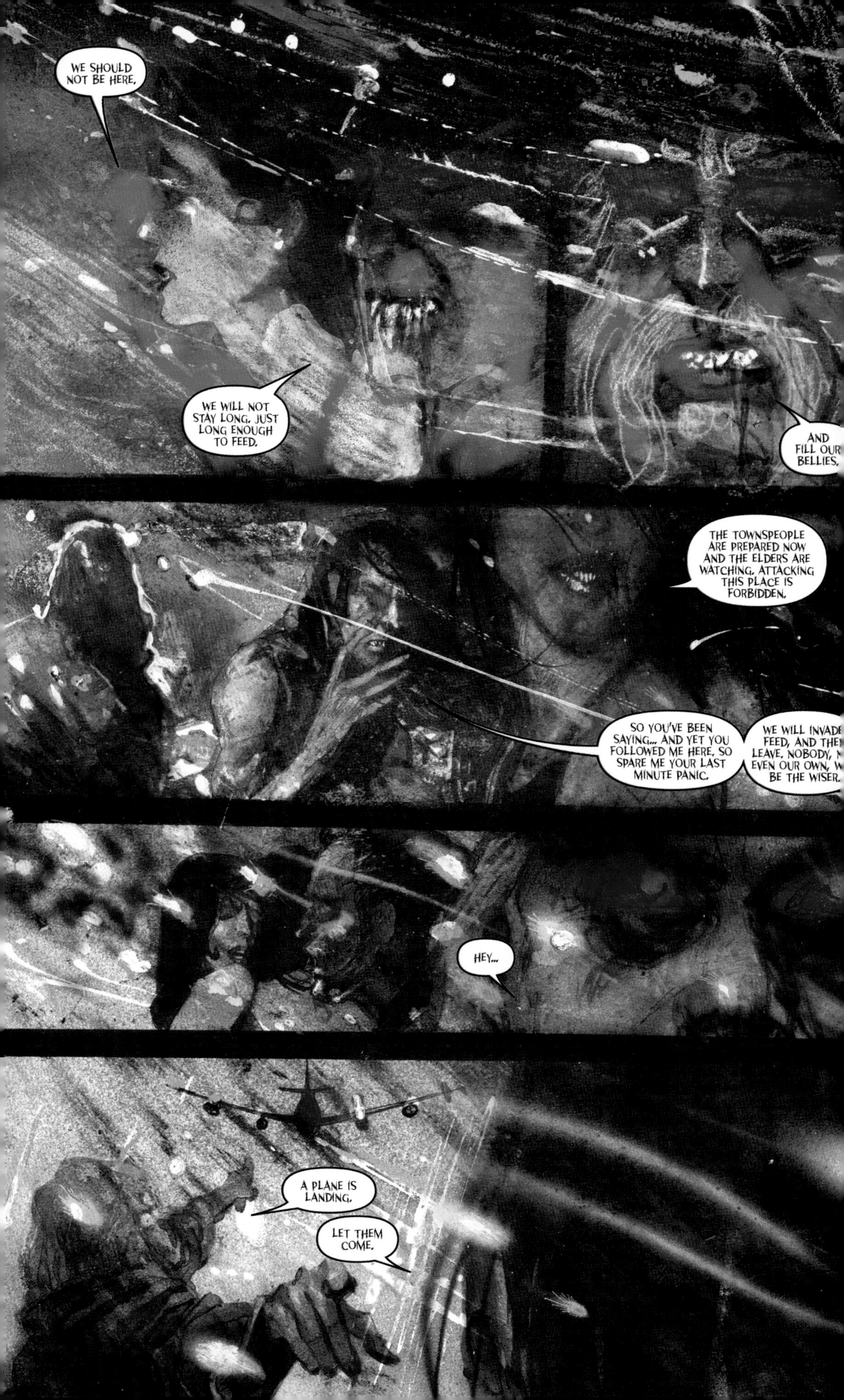
WE SHOULD NOT BE HERE.
WE WILL NOT STAY LONG. JUST LONG ENOUGH TO FEED.
AND FILL OUR BELLIES.
THE TOWNSPEOPLE ARE PREPARED NOW AND THE ELDERS ARE WATCHING. ATTACKING THIS PLACE IS FORBIDDEN.
SO YOU'VE BEEN SAYING... AND YET YOU FOLLOWED ME HERE, SO SPARE ME YOUR LAST MINUTE PANIC.
WE WILL INVADE FEED, AND THE LEAVE. NOBODY, EVEN OUR OWN, BE THE WISER.
HEY...
A PLANE IS LANDING.
LET THEM COME.

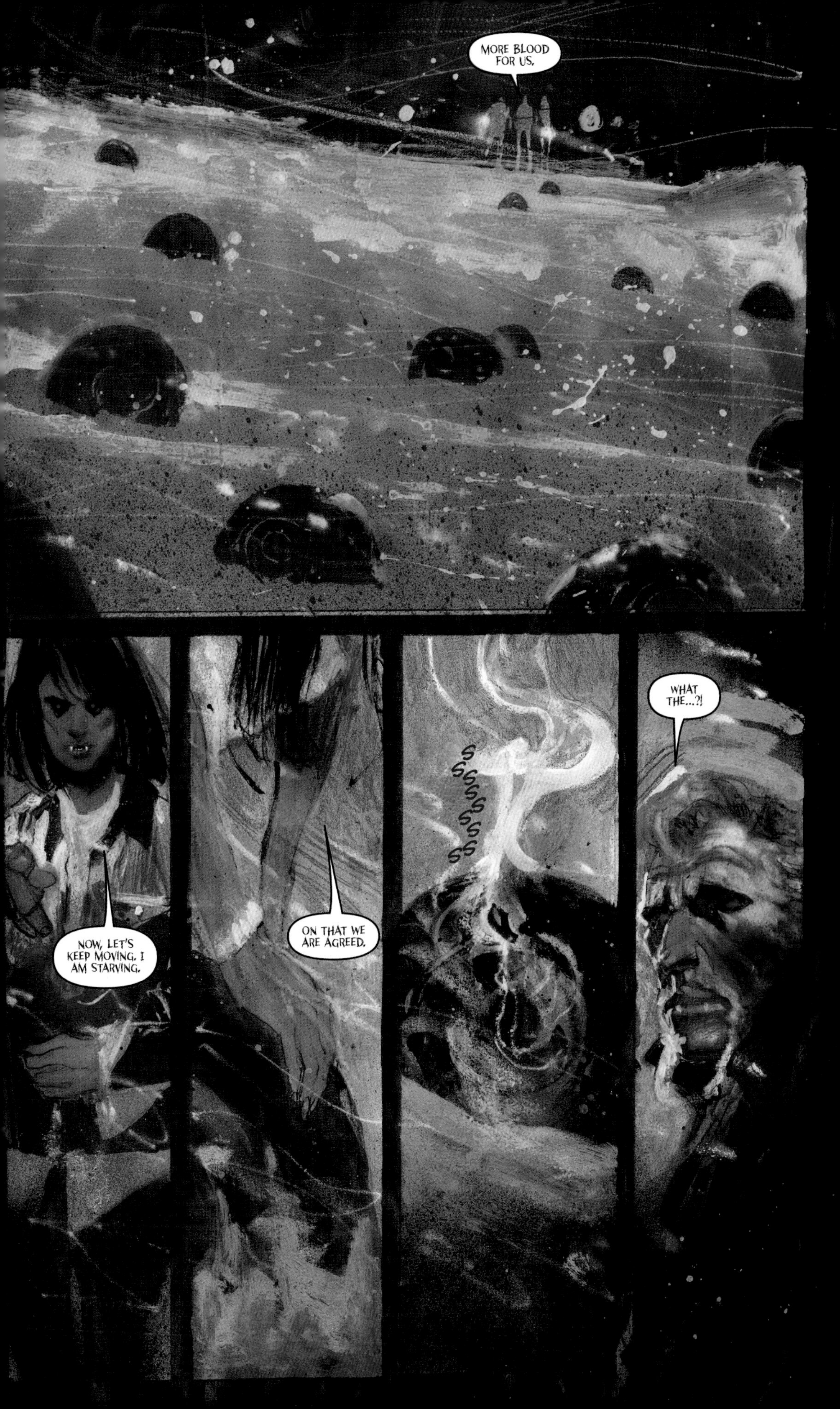
MORE BLOOD FOR US.
NOW, LET'S KEEP MOVING. I AM STARVING.
ON THAT WE ARE AGREED.
SSSSSSS
WHAT THE...?!

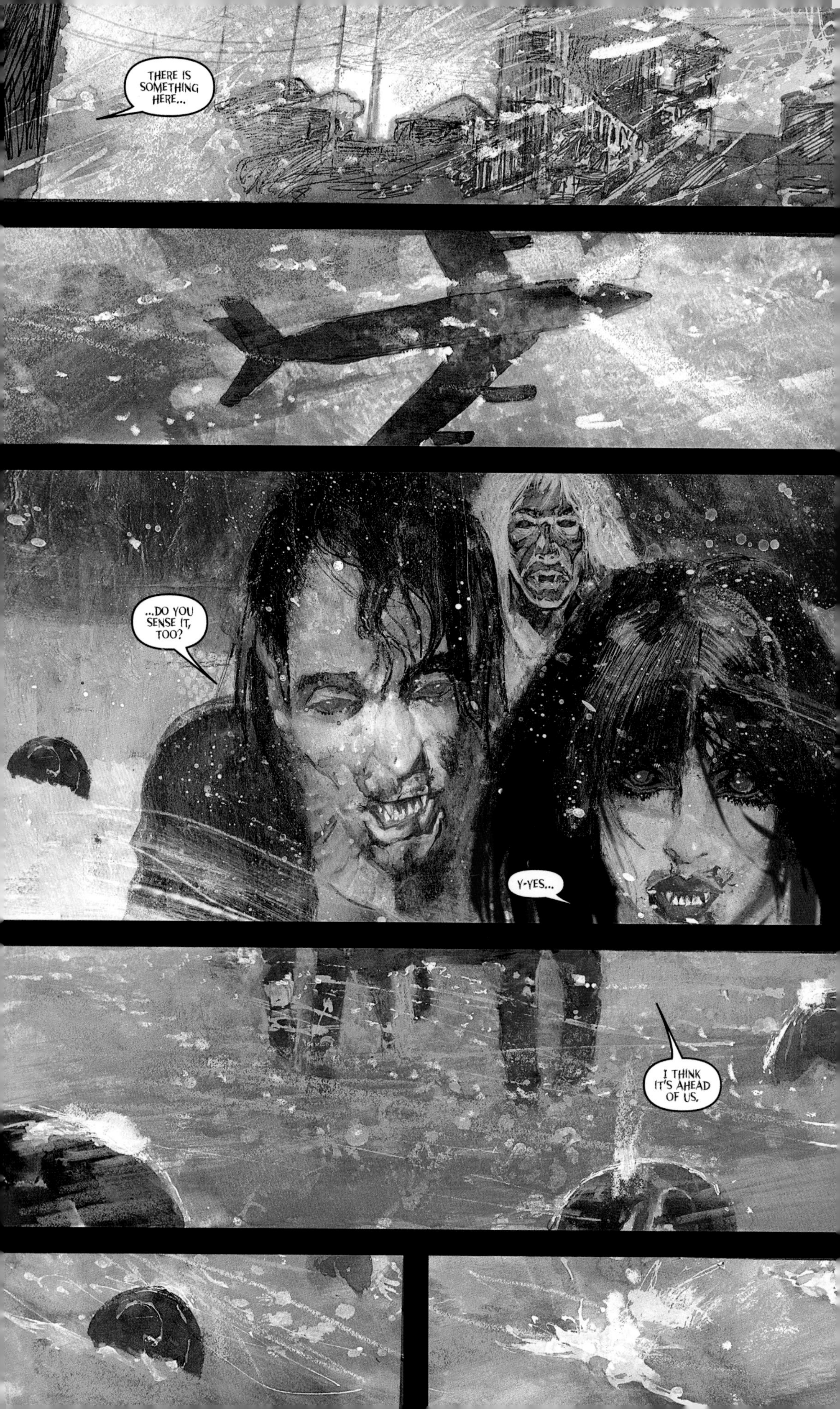
THERE IS SOMETHING HERE...
...DO YOU SENSE IT, TOO?
Y-YES...
I THINK IT'S AHEAD OF US.

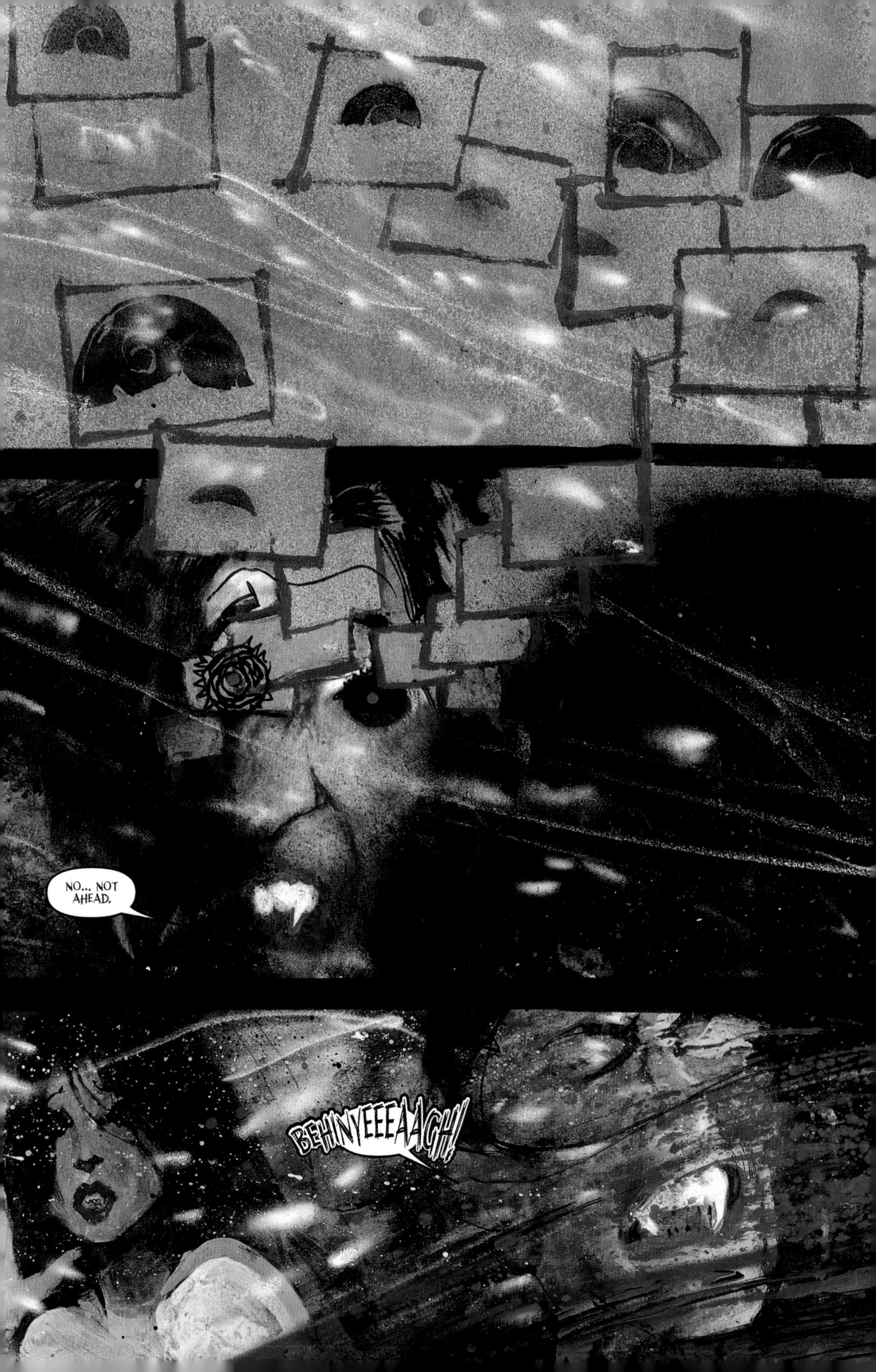
NO... NOT AHEAD.
BEHINYEEEAAGH!

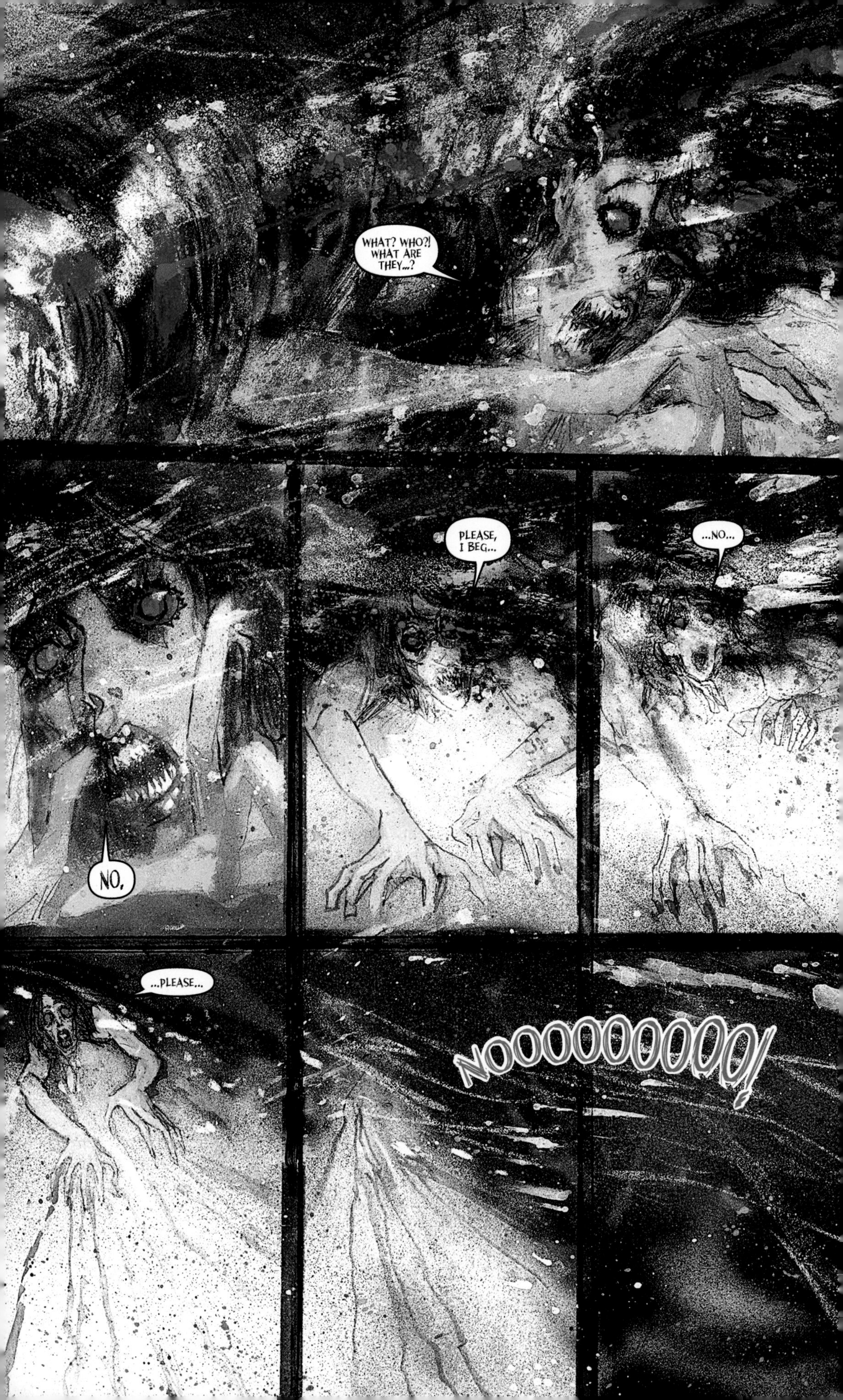
WHAT? WHO?! WHAT ARE THEY...?
NO,
PLEASE, I BEG...
...NO...
...PLEASE...
NOOOOOOOOO!

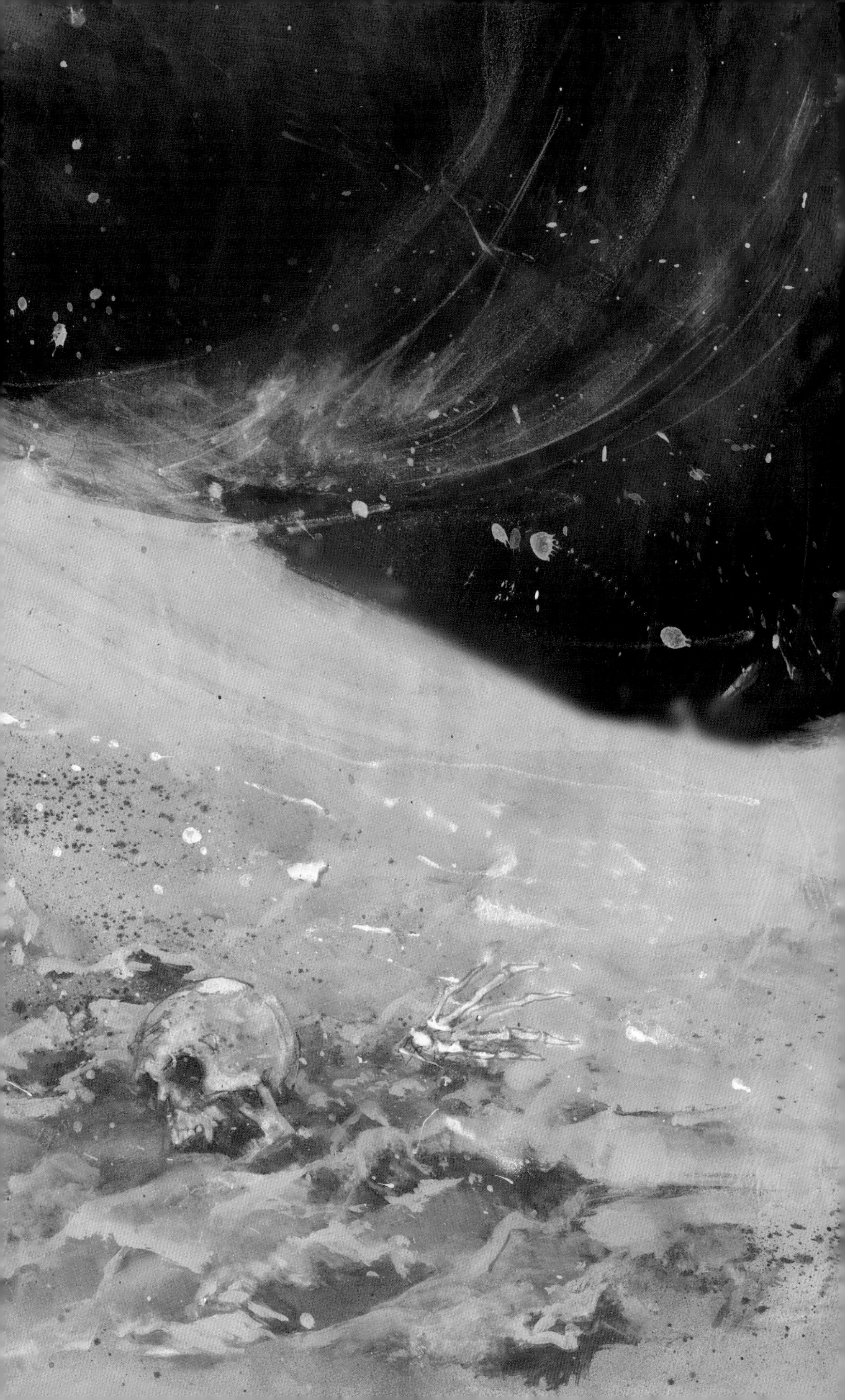

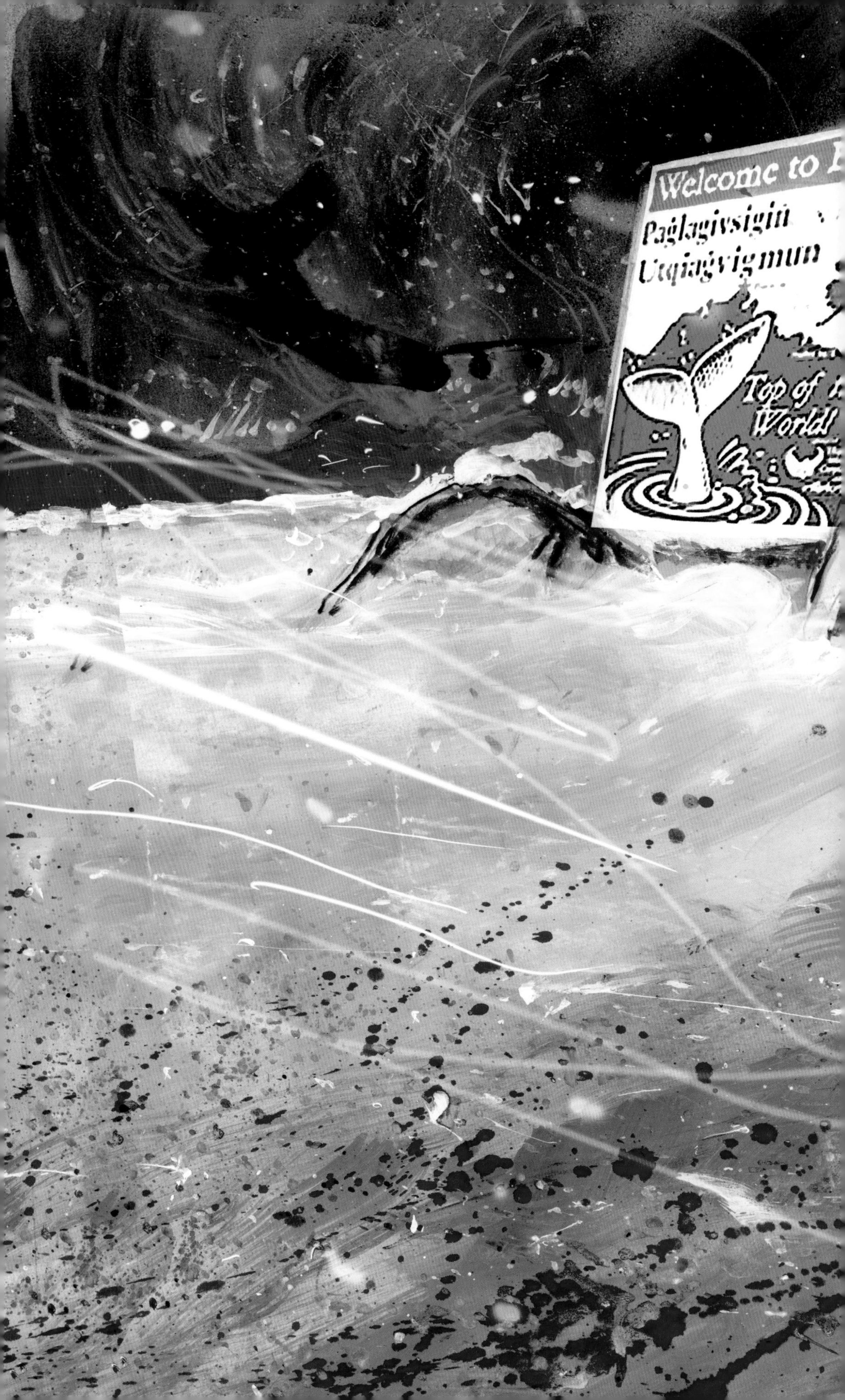
Welcome to
Paġlagivsigin
Utqiaġvigmun
Top of
World!

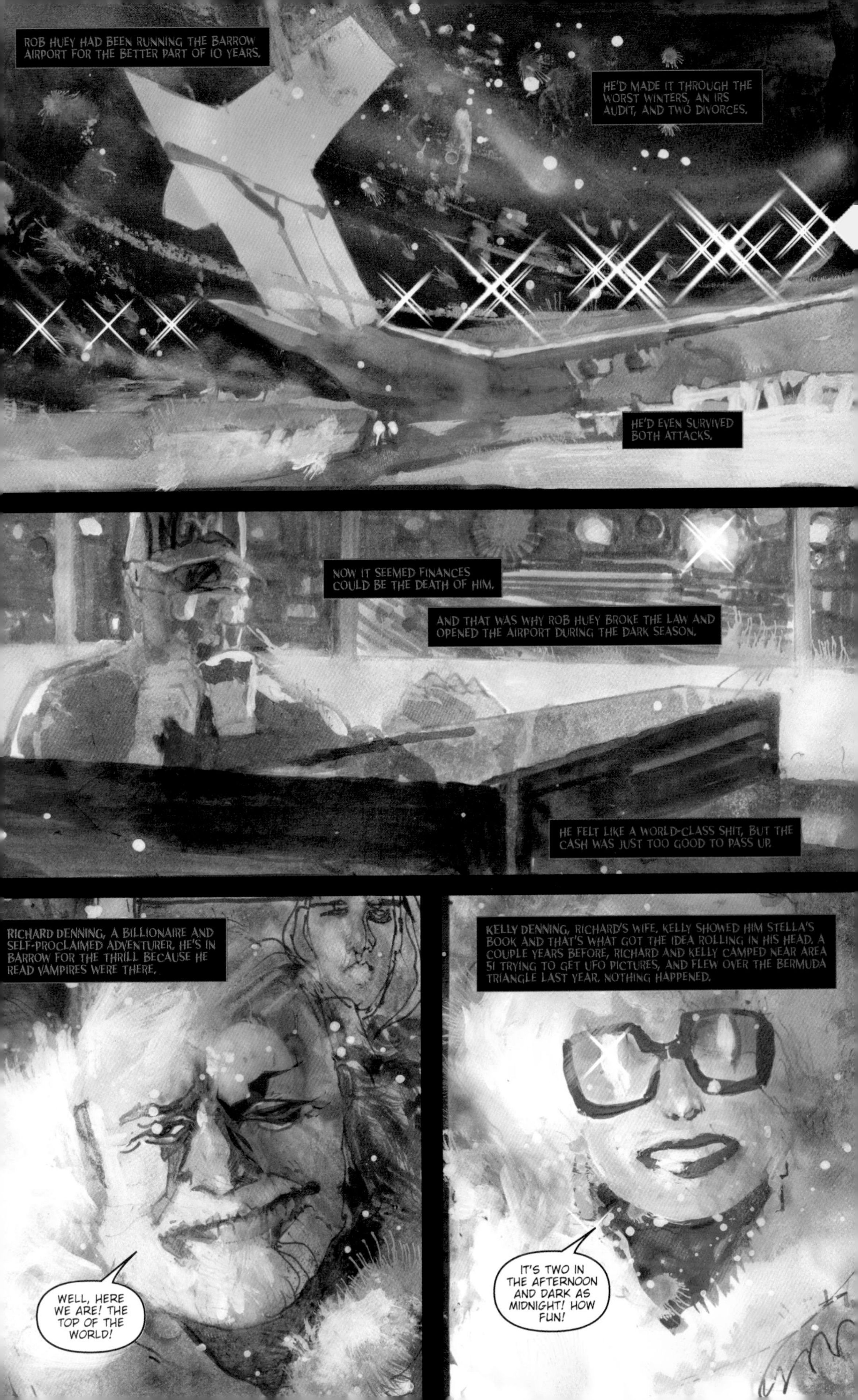
ROB HUEY HAD BEEN RUNNING THE BARROW AIRPORT FOR THE BETTER PART OF 10 YEARS.
HE'D MADE IT THROUGH THE WORST WINTERS, AN IRS AUDIT, AND TWO DIVORCES.
HE'D EVEN SURVIVED BOTH ATTACKS.
NOW IT SEEMED FINANCES COULD BE THE DEATH OF HIM.
AND THAT WAS WHY ROB HUEY BROKE THE LAW AND OPENED THE AIRPORT DURING THE DARK SEASON.
HE FELT LIKE A WORLD-CLASS SHIT, BUT THE CASH WAS JUST TOO GOOD TO PASS UP.
RICHARD DENNING, A BILLIONAIRE AND SELF-PROCLAIMED ADVENTURER, HE'S IN BARROW FOR THE THRILL BECAUSE HE READ VAMPIRES WERE THERE.
WELL, HERE WE ARE! THE TOP OF THE WORLD!
KELLY DENNING, RICHARD'S WIFE, KELLY SHOWED HIM STELLA'S BOOK AND THAT'S WHAT GOT THE IDEA ROLLING IN HIS HEAD. A COUPLE YEARS BEFORE, RICHARD AND KELLY CAMPED NEAR AREA 51 TRYING TO GET UFO PICTURES, AND FLEW OVER THE BERMUDA TRIANGLE LAST YEAR. NOTHING HAPPENED.
IT'S TWO IN THE AFTERNOON AND DARK AS MIDNIGHT! HOW FUN!

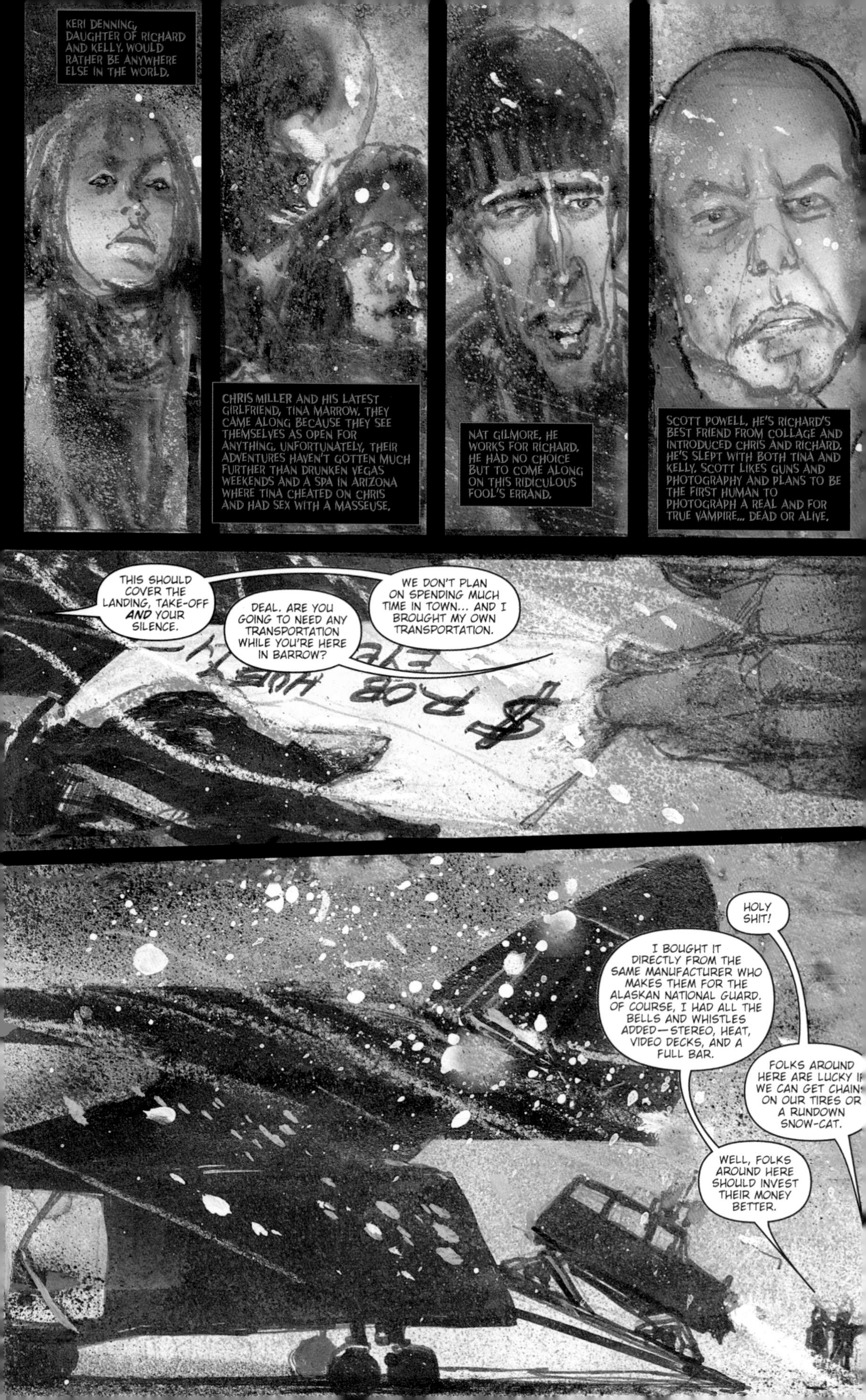
KERI DENNING, DAUGHTER OF RICHARD AND KELLY, WOULD RATHER BE ANYWHERE ELSE IN THE WORLD.
CHRIS MILLER AND HIS LATEST GIRLFRIEND, TINA MARROW, THEY CAME ALONG BECAUSE THEY SEE THEMSELVES AS OPEN FOR ANYTHING. UNFORTUNATELY, THEIR ADVENTURES HAVEN'T GOTTEN MUCH FURTHER THAN DRUNKEN VEGAS WEEKENDS AND A SPA IN ARIZONA WHERE TINA CHEATED ON CHRIS AND HAD SEX WITH A MASSEUSE.
NAT GILMORE, HE WORKS FOR RICHARD. HE HAD NO CHOICE BUT TO COME ALONG ON THIS RIDICULOUS FOOL'S ERRAND.
SCOTT POWELL, HE'S RICHARD'S BEST FRIEND FROM COLLAGE AND INTRODUCED CHRIS AND RICHARD. HE'S SLEPT WITH BOTH TINA AND KELLY. SCOTT LIKES GUNS AND PHOTOGRAPHY AND PLANS TO BE THE FIRST HUMAN TO PHOTOGRAPH A REAL AND FOR TRUE VAMPIRE... DEAD OR ALIVE.
THIS SHOULD COVER THE LANDING, TAKE-OFF **AND** YOUR SILENCE.
DEAL. ARE YOU GOING TO NEED ANY TRANSPORTATION WHILE YOU'RE HERE IN BARROW?
WE DON'T PLAN ON SPENDING MUCH TIME IN TOWN... AND I BROUGHT MY OWN TRANSPORTATION.
HOLY SHIT!
I BOUGHT IT DIRECTLY FROM THE SAME MANUFACTURER WHO MAKES THEM FOR THE ALASKAN NATIONAL GUARD. OF COURSE, I HAD ALL THE BELLS AND WHISTLES ADDED—STEREO, HEAT, VIDEO DECKS, AND A FULL BAR.
FOLKS AROUND HERE ARE LUCKY IF WE CAN GET CHAINS ON OUR TIRES OR A RUNDOWN SNOW-CAT.
WELL, FOLKS AROUND HERE SHOULD INVEST THEIR MONEY BETTER.

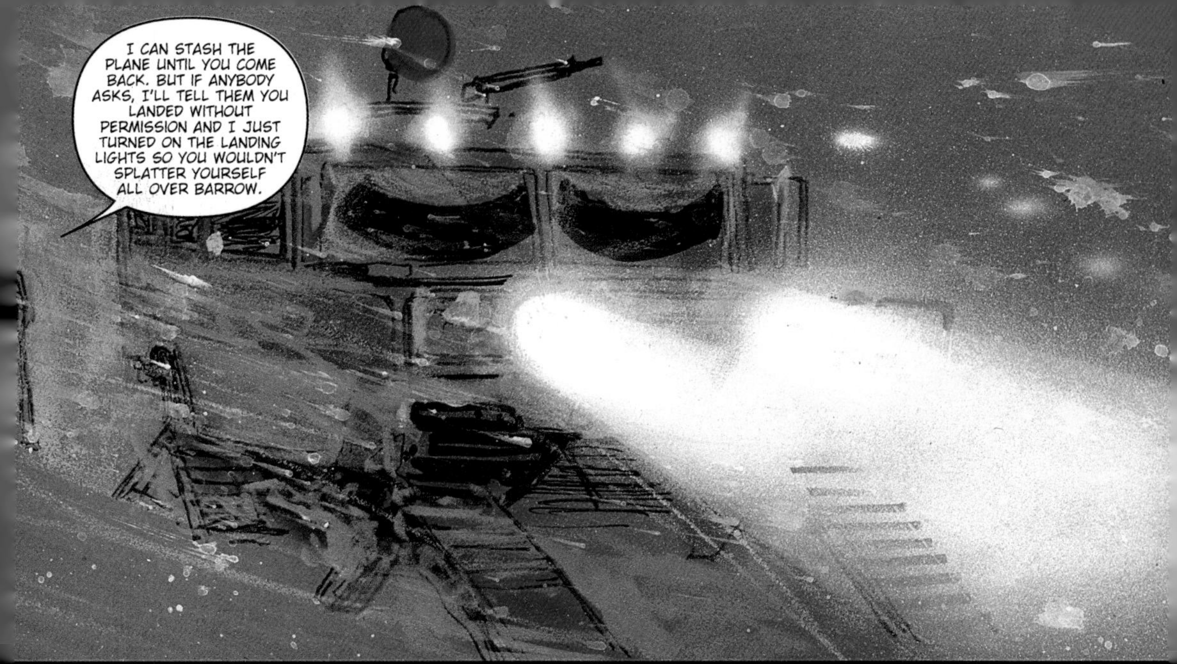
I CAN STASH THE PLANE UNTIL YOU COME BACK. BUT IF ANYBODY ASKS, I'LL TELL THEM YOU LANDED WITHOUT PERMISSION AND I JUST TURNED ON THE LANDING LIGHTS SO YOU WOULDN'T SPLATTER YOURSELF ALL OVER BARROW.

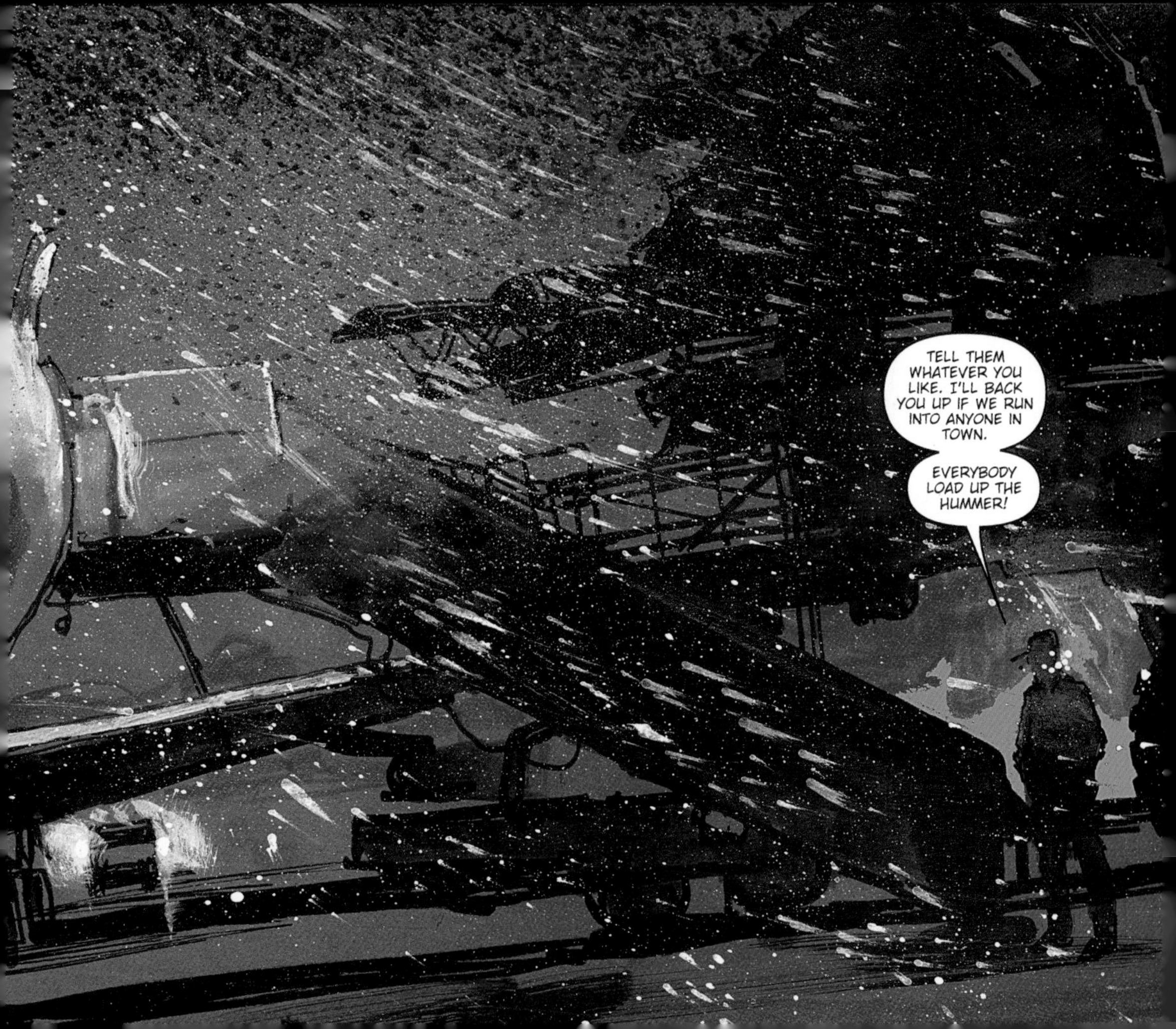
TELL THEM WHATEVER YOU LIKE. I'LL BACK YOU UP IF WE RUN INTO ANYONE IN TOWN.
EVERYBODY LOAD UP THE HUMMER!

TOWN? YOU SAID YOU WEREN'T GOING INTO TOWN. BARROW IS IN LOCKDOWN. YOU SHOW UP AT THE GATES AND THEY'LL KNOW I LET YOU LAND!

ALL ROB HUEY CAN DO IS STAND THERE WITH A FISTFUL OF CASH AND WONDER IF IT'S WORTH IT.

AND THAT, MY FRIEND, IS WHERE WE TELL YOUR LIE AND COVER YOUR ASS.

EVEN HE KNOWS DEEP DOWN IF THESE JACKASSES GO ANYWHERE BUT BARROW, THEY'LL PROBABLY WIND UP DEAD.

IF THE COLD DIDN'T GET THEM...

NOT THAT I WANT TO GIVE THAT WHELP AT THE AIRPORT ANY ADDED HELP, BUT I DON'T CARE IF WE GO INTO BARROW OR NOT. IT'S TOO WELL-PROTECTED. IF WE'RE GOING TO FIND ANY REAL ACTION, IT'S GOING TO BE OUTSIDE THE FENCES.

BUT YOU PROMISED! KERI AND I WANT TO PHOTOGRAPH EBEN OLEMAUN'S GRAVE AND THE REMAINS OF IKOS DINER.

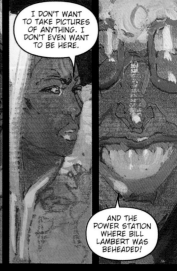

I DON'T WANT TO TAKE PICTURES OF ANYTHING. I DON'T WANT TO BE HERE.

AND THE POWER STATION WHERE BILL LAMBERT WAS BEHEADED!

I BELIEVE HIS NAME WAS *GUS* LAMBERT, MRS. DENNING.

WHATEVER. WE SHOULD DOCUMENT AS MUCH AS WE CAN SO IF WE DO GET ANY REAL PROOF, WE'LL HAVE EVERYTHING WE NEED.

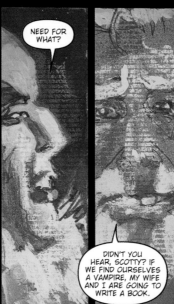

NEED FOR WHAT?

DIDN'T YOU HEAR, SCOTTY? IF WE FIND OURSELVES A VAMPIRE, MY WIFE AND I ARE GOING TO WRITE A BOOK.

MILLIONAIRE, VAMPIRE-HUNTER, AUTHOR.

THAT'S *BILLIONAIRE*, NAT, THANK YOU VERY MUCH.

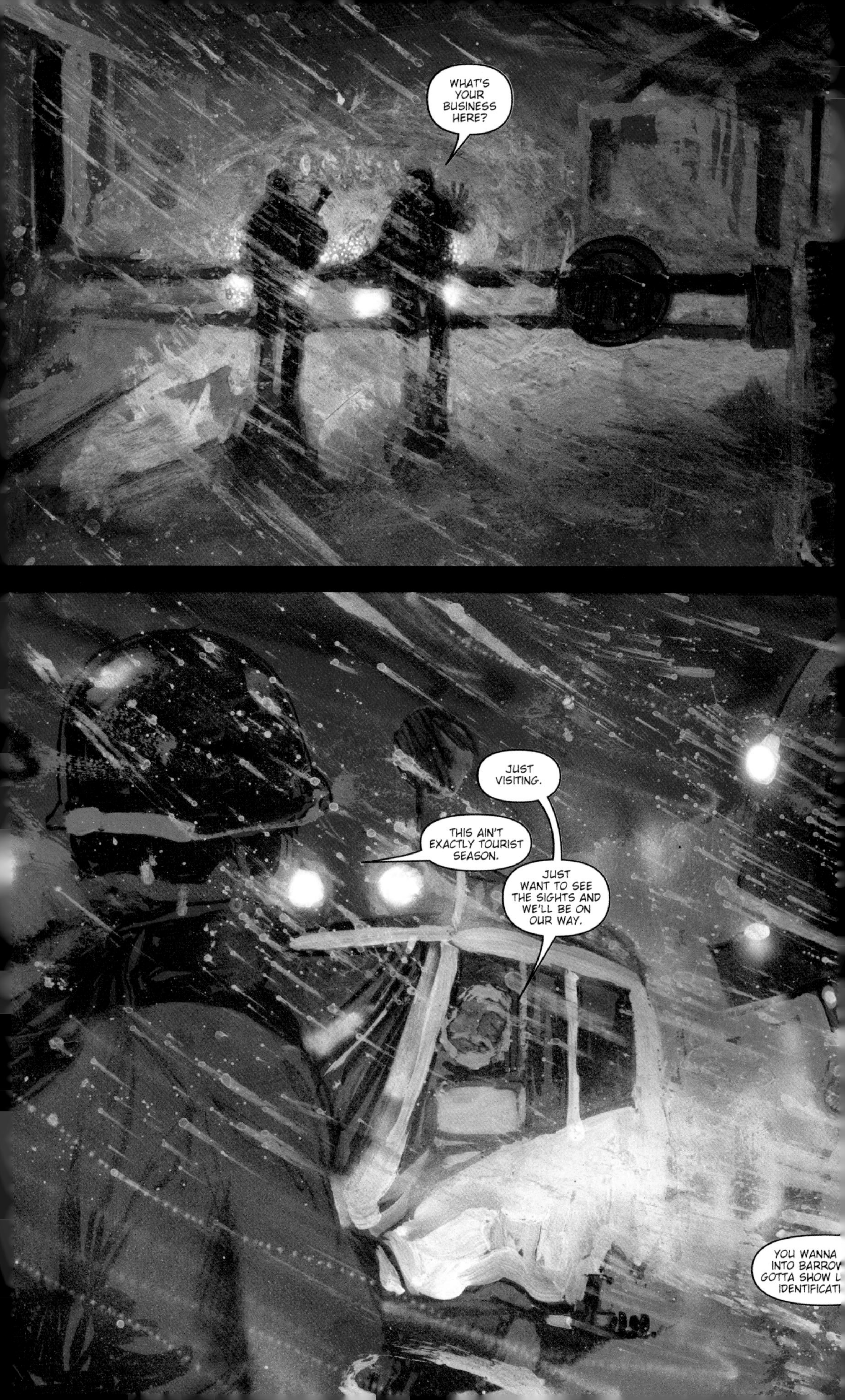
WHAT'S YOUR BUSINESS HERE?
JUST VISITING.
THIS AIN'T EXACTLY TOURIST SEASON.
JUST WANT TO SEE THE SIGHTS AND WE'LL BE ON OUR WAY.
YOU WANNA INTO BARROW GOTTA SHOW L IDENTIFICATI

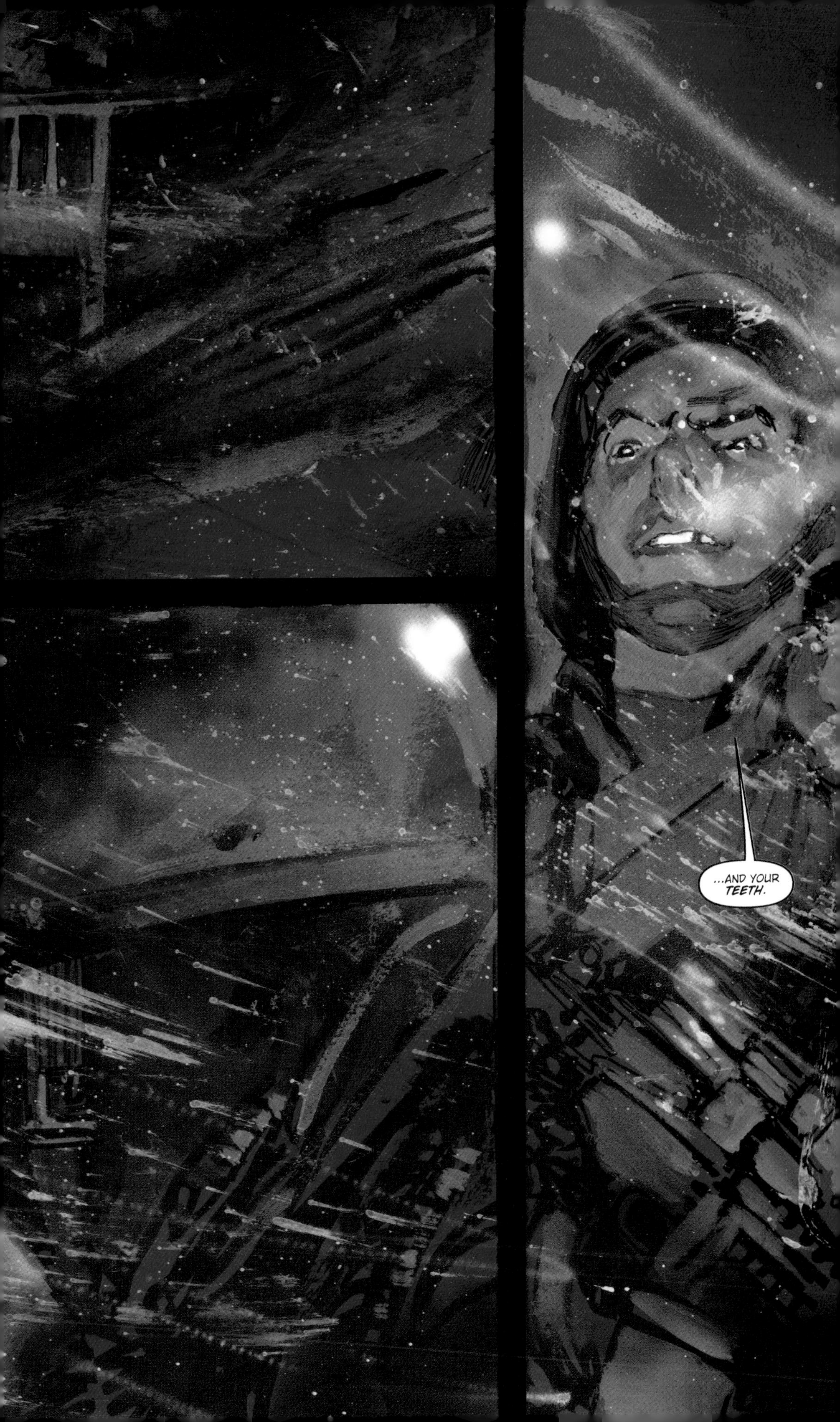
...AND YOUR TEETH.

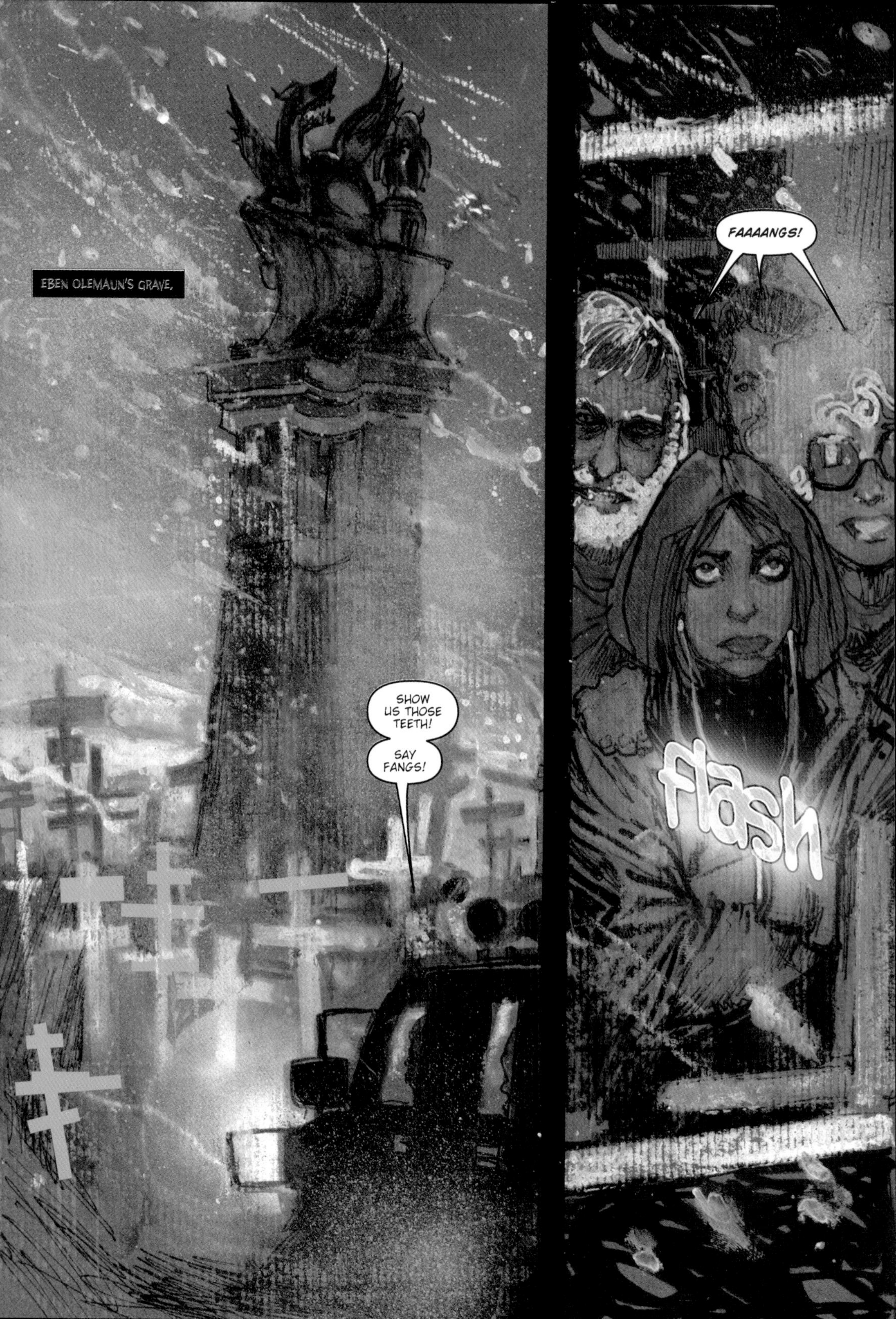
EBEN OLEMAUN'S GRAVE.
SHOW US THOSE TEETH!
SAY FANGS!
FAAAANGS!
flash

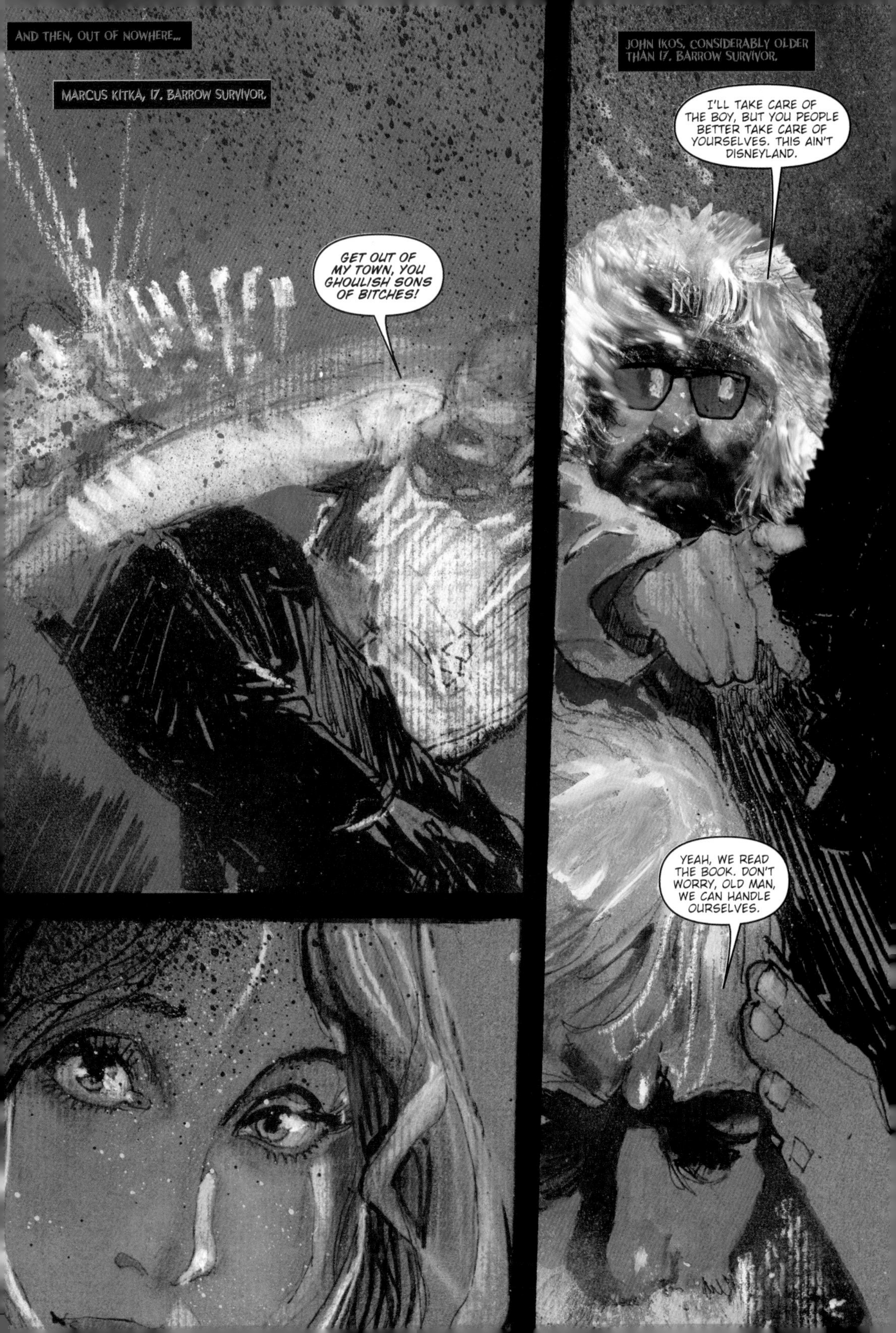

AND THEN, OUT OF NOWHERE...
MARCUS KITKA, 17. BARROW SURVIVOR.
GET OUT OF MY TOWN, YOU GHOULISH SONS OF BITCHES!
JOHN IKOS, CONSIDERABLY OLDER THAN 17. BARROW SURVIVOR.
I'LL TAKE CARE OF THE BOY, BUT YOU PEOPLE BETTER TAKE CARE OF YOURSELVES. THIS AIN'T DISNEYLAND.
YEAH, WE READ THE BOOK. DON'T WORRY, OLD MAN, WE CAN HANDLE OURSELVES.

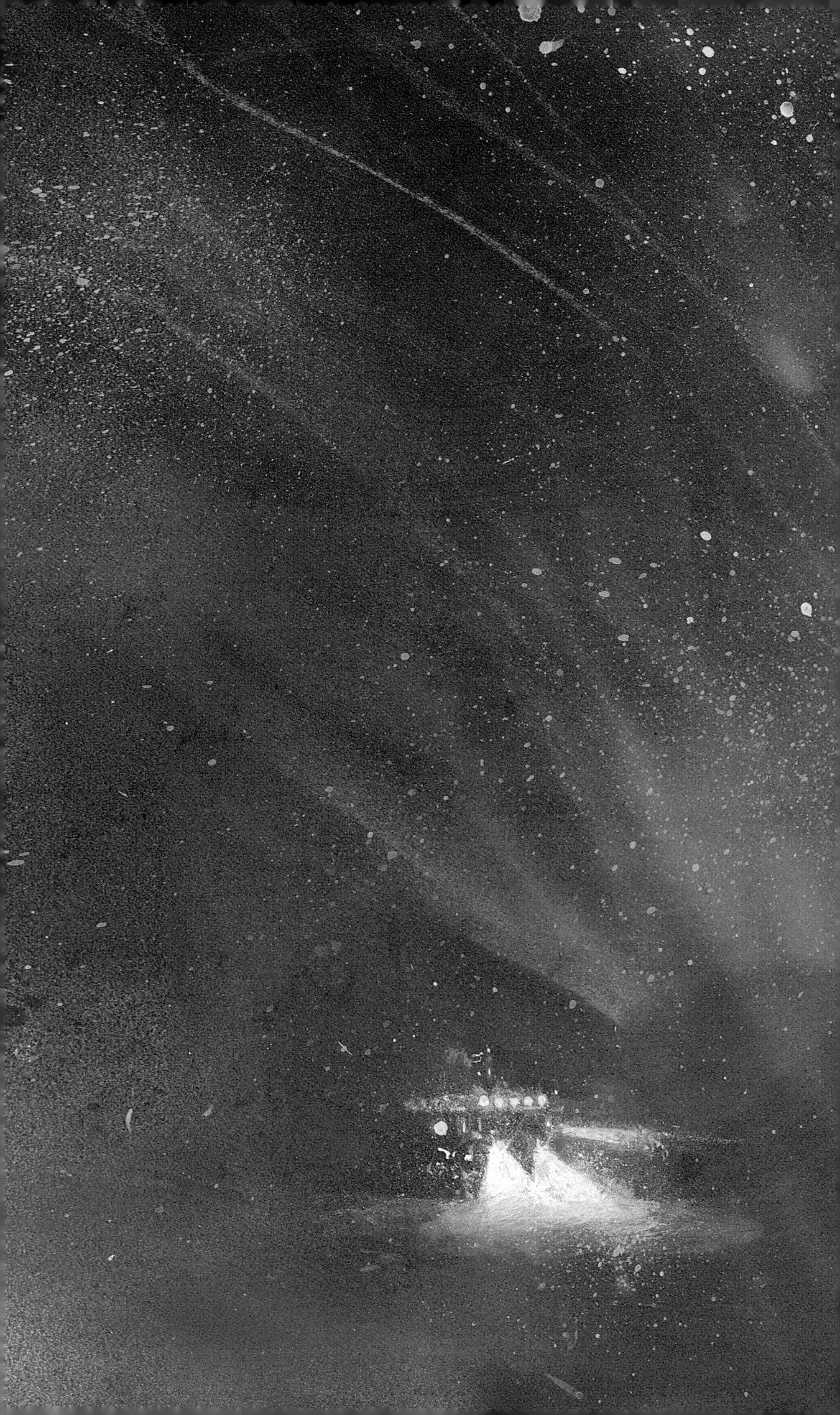

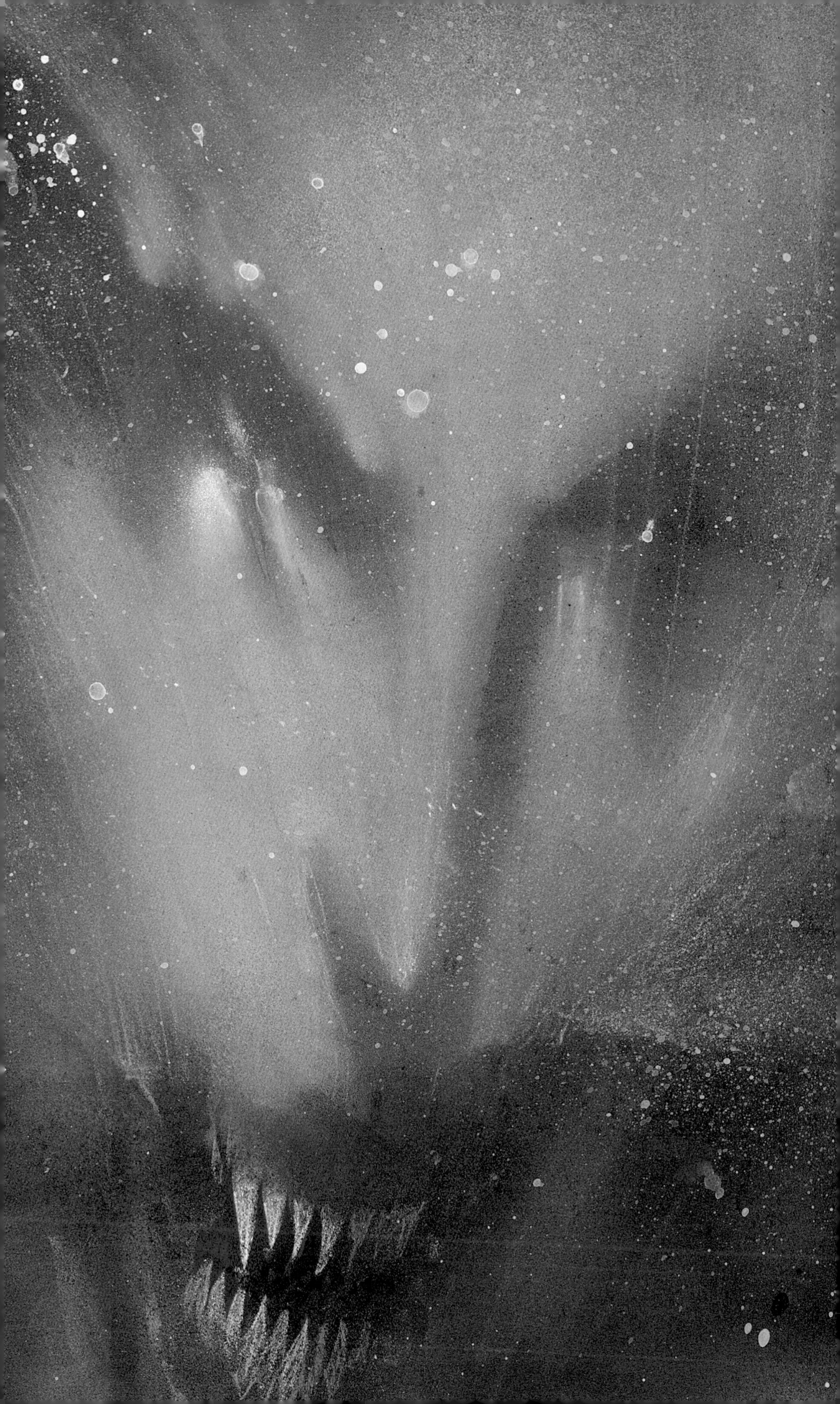

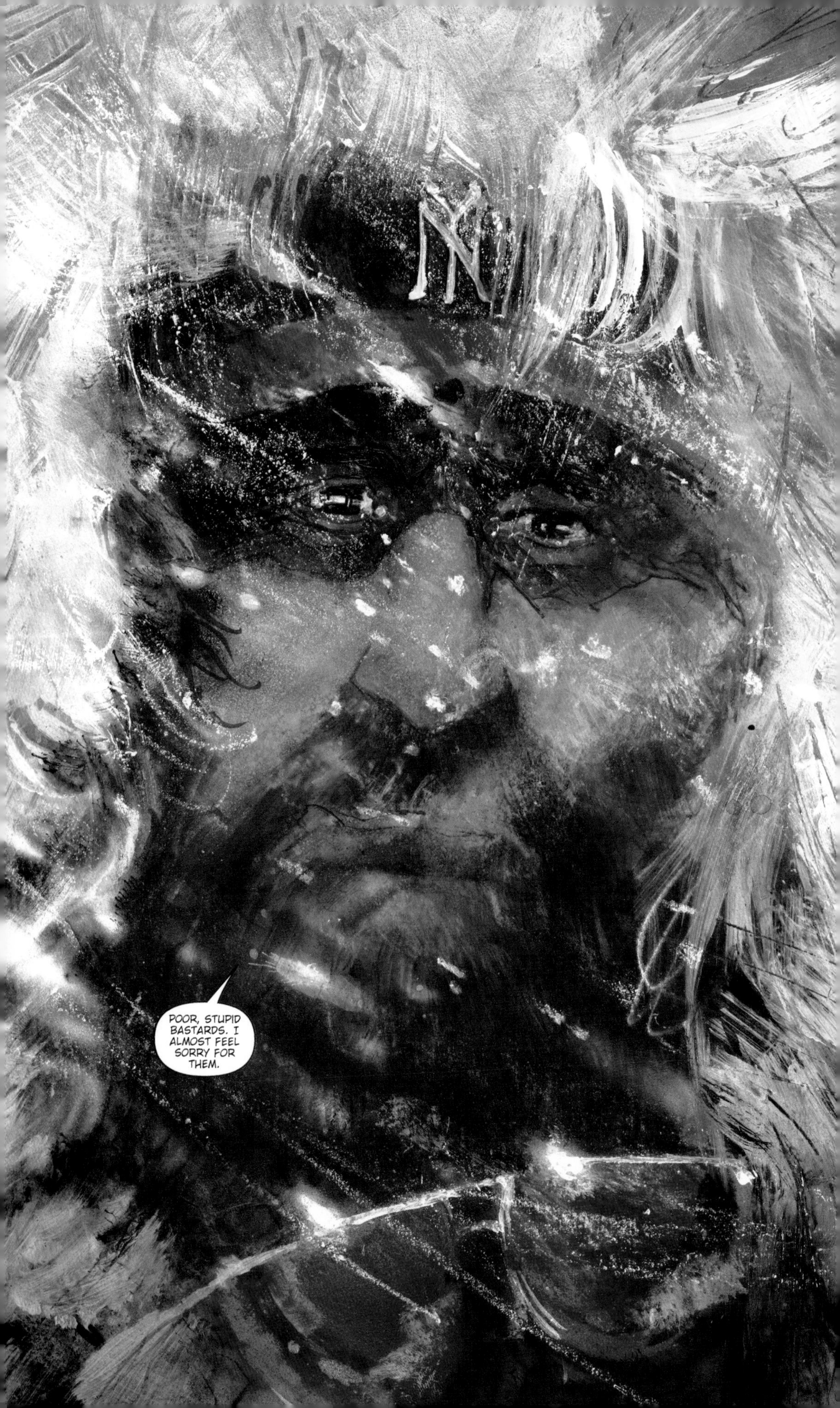
POOR, STUPID BASTARDS. I ALMOST FEEL SORRY FOR THEM.

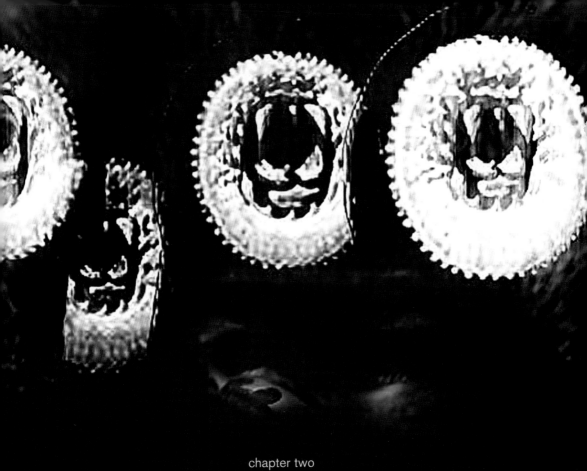

chapter two

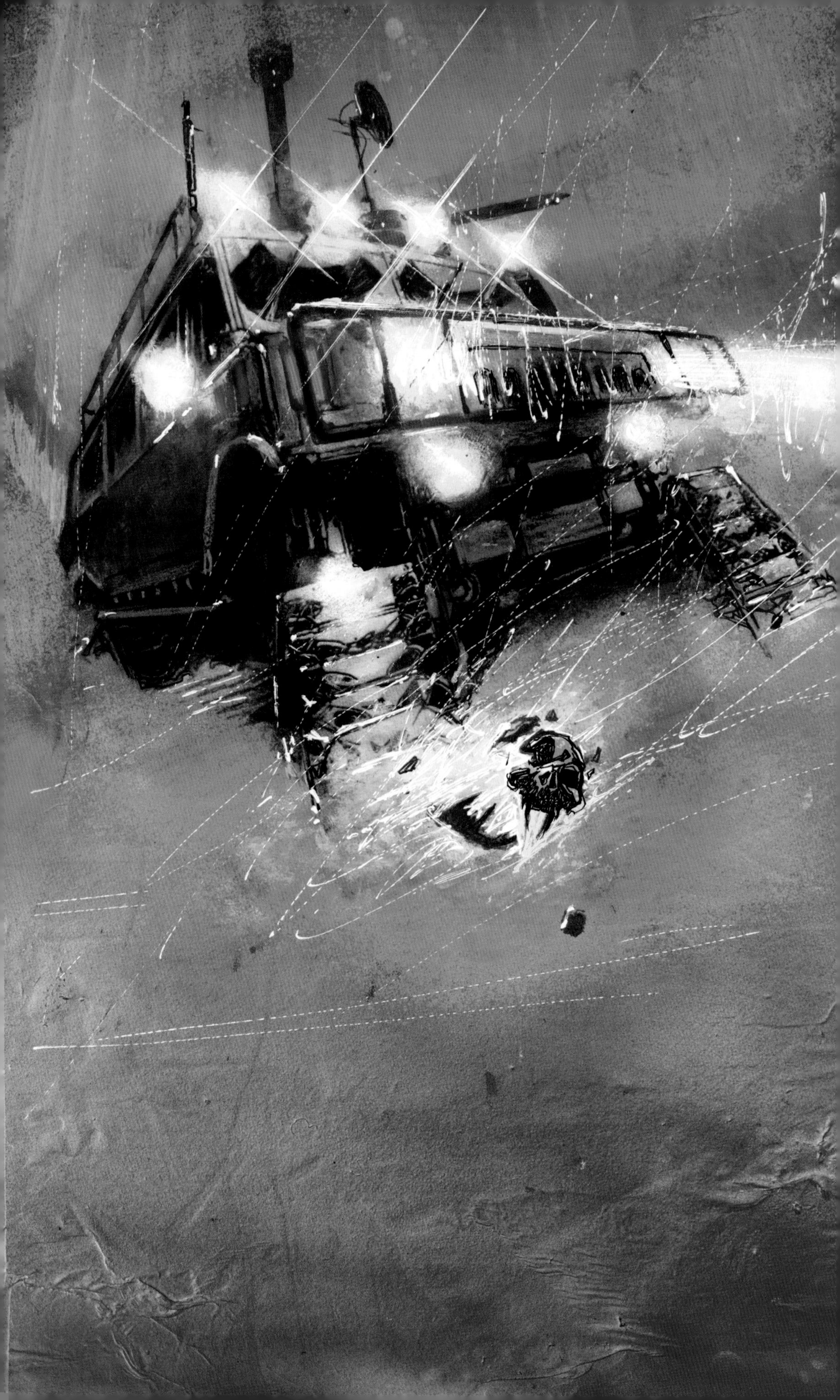

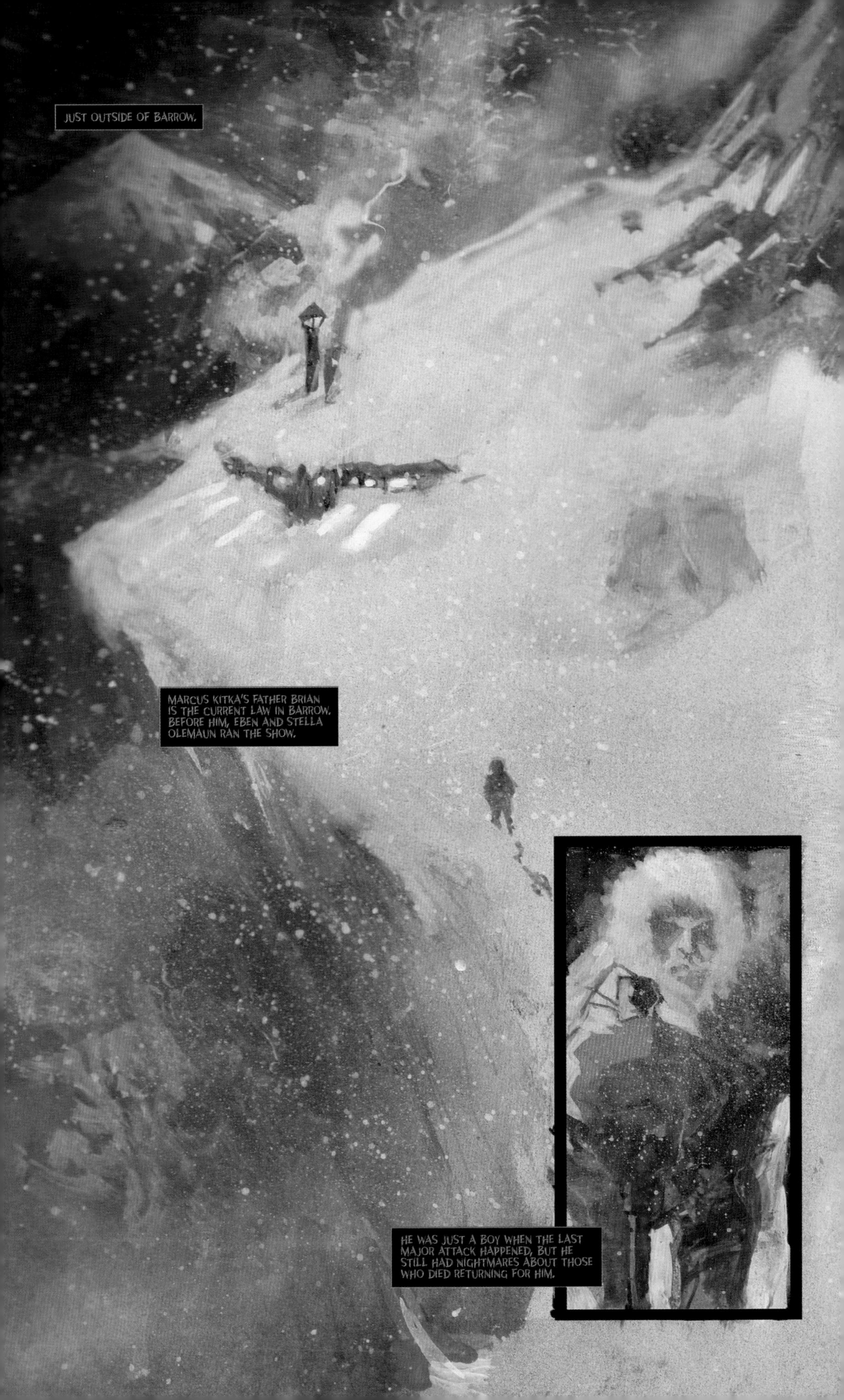
JUST OUTSIDE OF BARROW.
MARCUS KITKA'S FATHER BRIAN IS THE CURRENT LAW IN BARROW. BEFORE HIM, EBEN AND STELLA OLEMAUN RAN THE SHOW.
HE WAS JUST A BOY WHEN THE LAST MAJOR ATTACK HAPPENED, BUT HE STILL HAD NIGHTMARES ABOUT THOSE WHO DIED RETURNING FOR HIM.

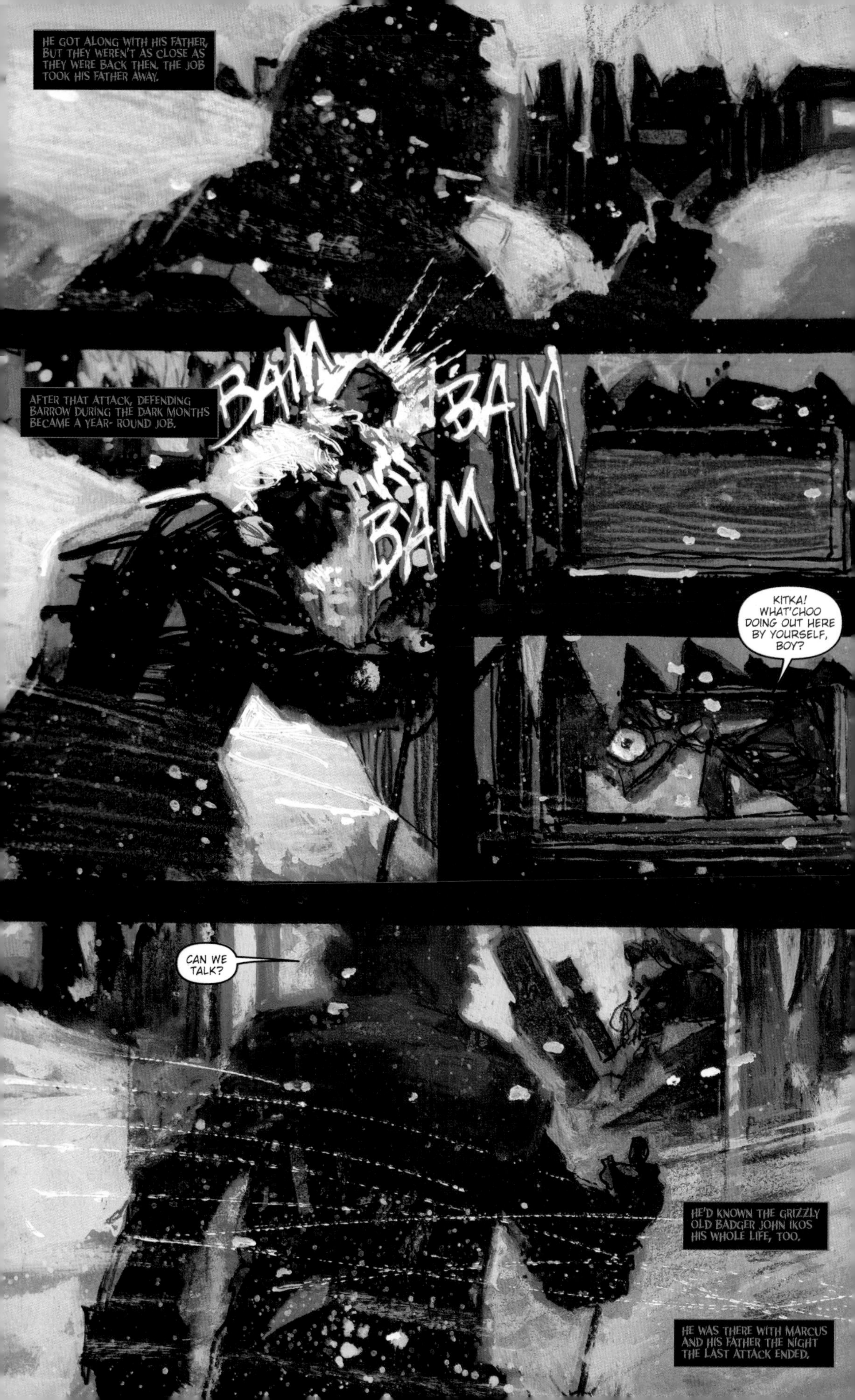
HE GOT ALONG WITH HIS FATHER, BUT THEY WEREN'T AS CLOSE AS THEY WERE BACK THEN. THE JOB TOOK HIS FATHER AWAY.
AFTER THAT ATTACK, DEFENDING BARROW DURING THE DARK MONTHS BECAME A YEAR- ROUND JOB.
BAM
BAM
BAM
KITKA! WHAT'CHOO DOING OUT HERE BY YOURSELF, BOY?
CAN WE TALK?
HE'D KNOWN THE GRIZZLY OLD BADGER JOHN IKOS HIS WHOLE LIFE, TOO.
HE WAS THERE WITH MARCUS AND HIS FATHER THE NIGHT THE LAST ATTACK ENDED.

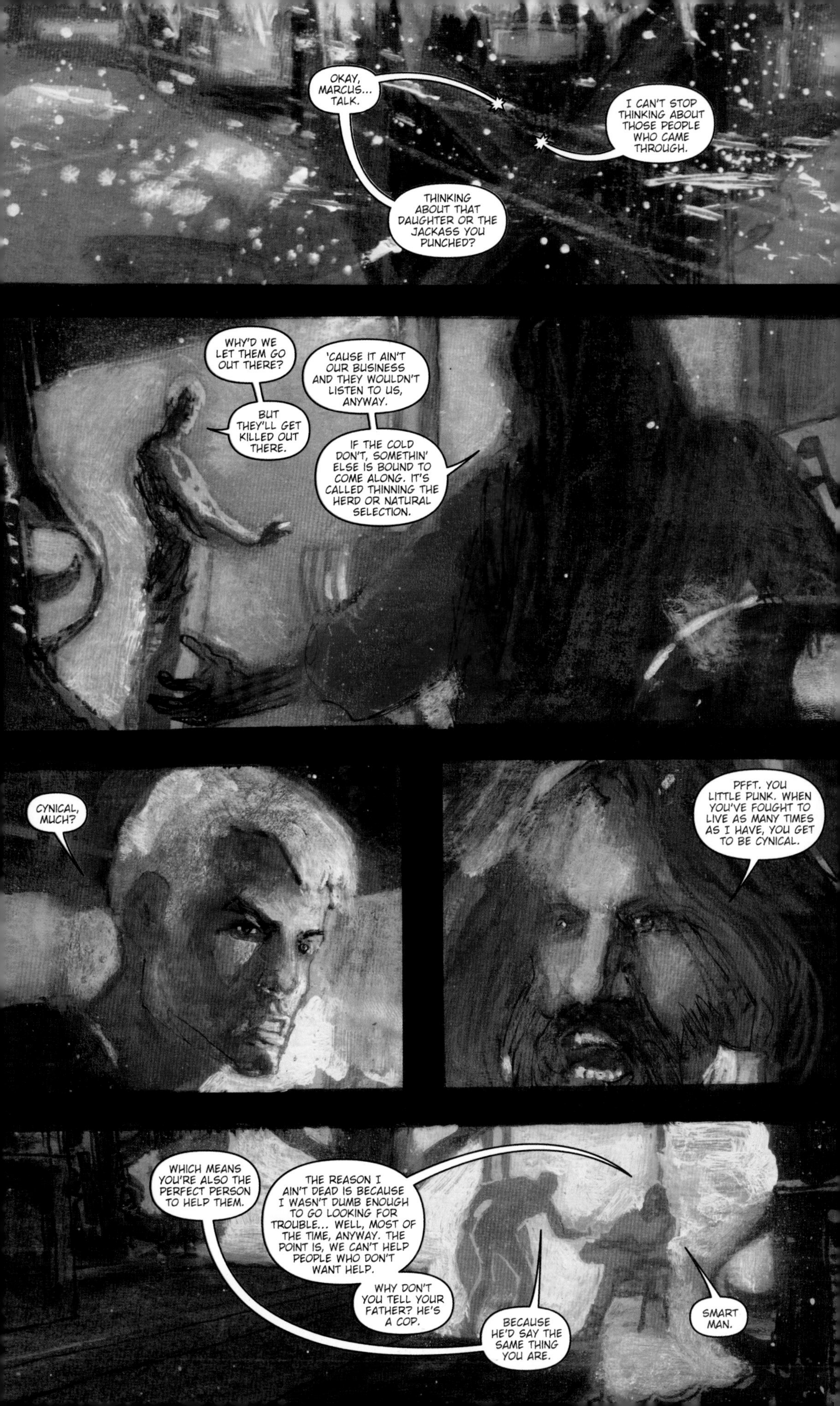

OKAY, MARCUS... TALK.
I CAN'T STOP THINKING ABOUT THOSE PEOPLE WHO CAME THROUGH.
THINKING ABOUT THAT DAUGHTER OR THE JACKASS YOU PUNCHED?
WHY'D WE LET THEM GO OUT THERE?
BUT THEY'LL GET KILLED OUT THERE.
'CAUSE IT AIN'T OUR BUSINESS AND THEY WOULDN'T LISTEN TO US, ANYWAY.
IF THE COLD DON'T, SOMETHIN' ELSE IS BOUND TO COME ALONG. IT'S CALLED THINNING THE HERD OR NATURAL SELECTION.
CYNICAL, MUCH?
PFFT. YOU LITTLE PUNK. WHEN YOU'VE FOUGHT TO LIVE AS MANY TIMES AS I HAVE, YOU GET TO BE CYNICAL.
THE REASON I AIN'T DEAD IS BECAUSE I WASN'T DUMB ENOUGH TO GO LOOKING FOR TROUBLE... WELL, MOST OF THE TIME, ANYWAY. THE POINT IS, WE CAN'T HELP PEOPLE WHO DON'T WANT HELP.
WHICH MEANS YOU'RE ALSO THE PERFECT PERSON TO HELP THEM.
WHY DON'T YOU TELL YOUR FATHER? HE'S A COP.
BECAUSE HE'D SAY THE SAME THING YOU ARE.
SMART MAN.

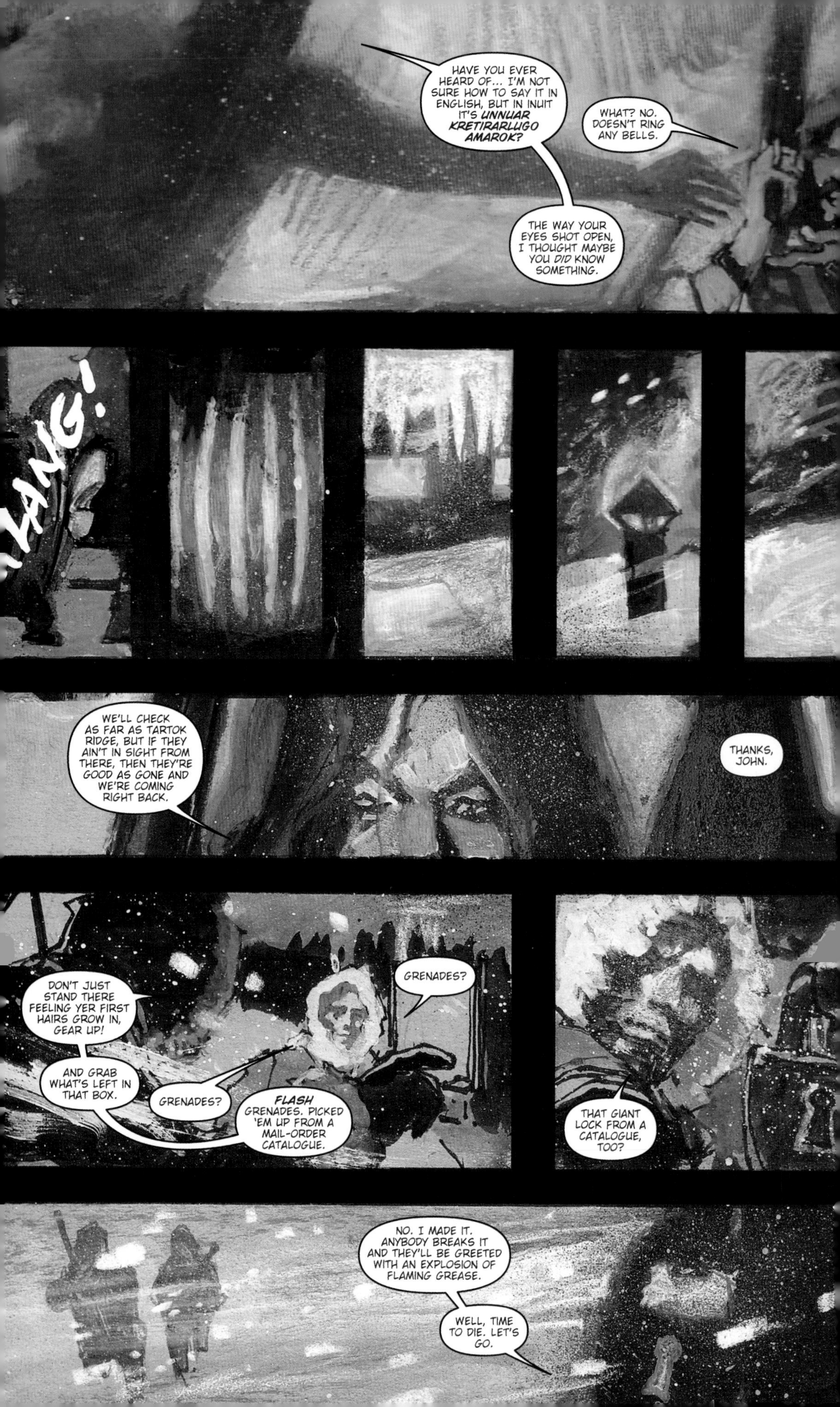

HAVE YOU EVER HEARD OF... I'M NOT SURE HOW TO SAY IT IN ENGLISH, BUT IN INUIT IT'S *UNNUAR KRETIRARLUGO AMAROK?*
WHAT? NO. DOESN'T RING ANY BELLS.
THE WAY YOUR EYES SHOT OPEN, I THOUGHT MAYBE YOU *DID* KNOW SOMETHING.
LANG!
WE'LL CHECK AS FAR AS TARTOK RIDGE, BUT IF THEY AIN'T IN SIGHT FROM THERE, THEN THEY'RE GOOD AS GONE AND WE'RE COMING RIGHT BACK.
THANKS, JOHN.
DON'T JUST STAND THERE FEELING YER FIRST HAIRS GROW IN, GEAR UP!
AND GRAB WHAT'S LEFT IN THAT BOX.
GRENADES?
GRENADES?
FLASH GRENADES. PICKED 'EM UP FROM A MAIL-ORDER CATALOGUE.
THAT GIANT LOCK FROM A CATALOGUE, TOO?
NO. I MADE IT. ANYBODY BREAKS IT AND THEY'LL BE GREETED WITH AN EXPLOSION OF FLAMING GREASE.
WELL, TIME TO DIE. LET'S GO.

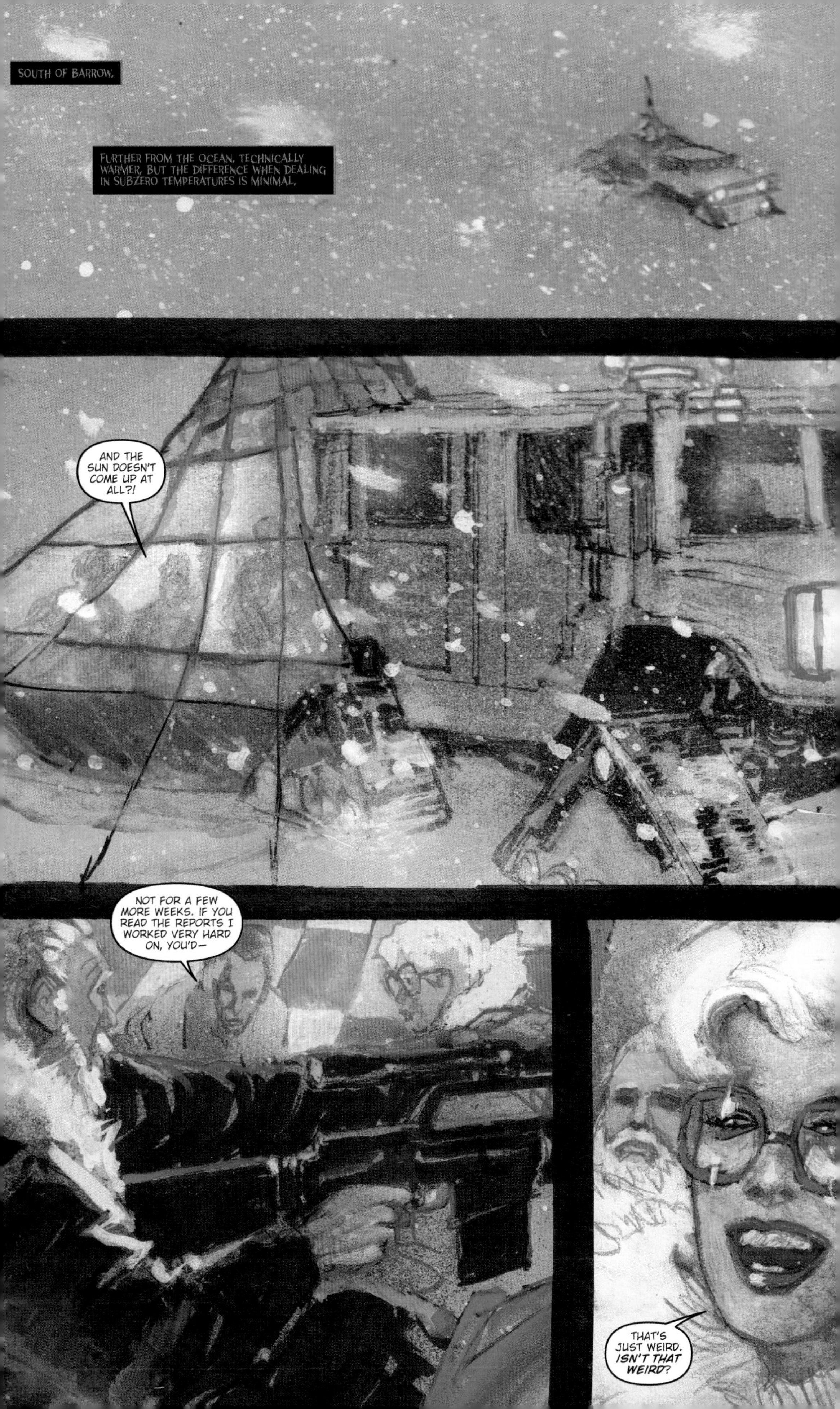
SOUTH OF BARROW.
FURTHER FROM THE OCEAN, TECHNICALLY WARMER, BUT THE DIFFERENCE WHEN DEALING IN SUBZERO TEMPERATURES IS MINIMAL.
AND THE SUN DOESN'T COME UP AT ALL?!
NOT FOR A FEW MORE WEEKS. IF YOU READ THE REPORTS I WORKED VERY HARD ON, YOU'D—
THAT'S JUST WEIRD. *ISN'T THAT WEIRD?*

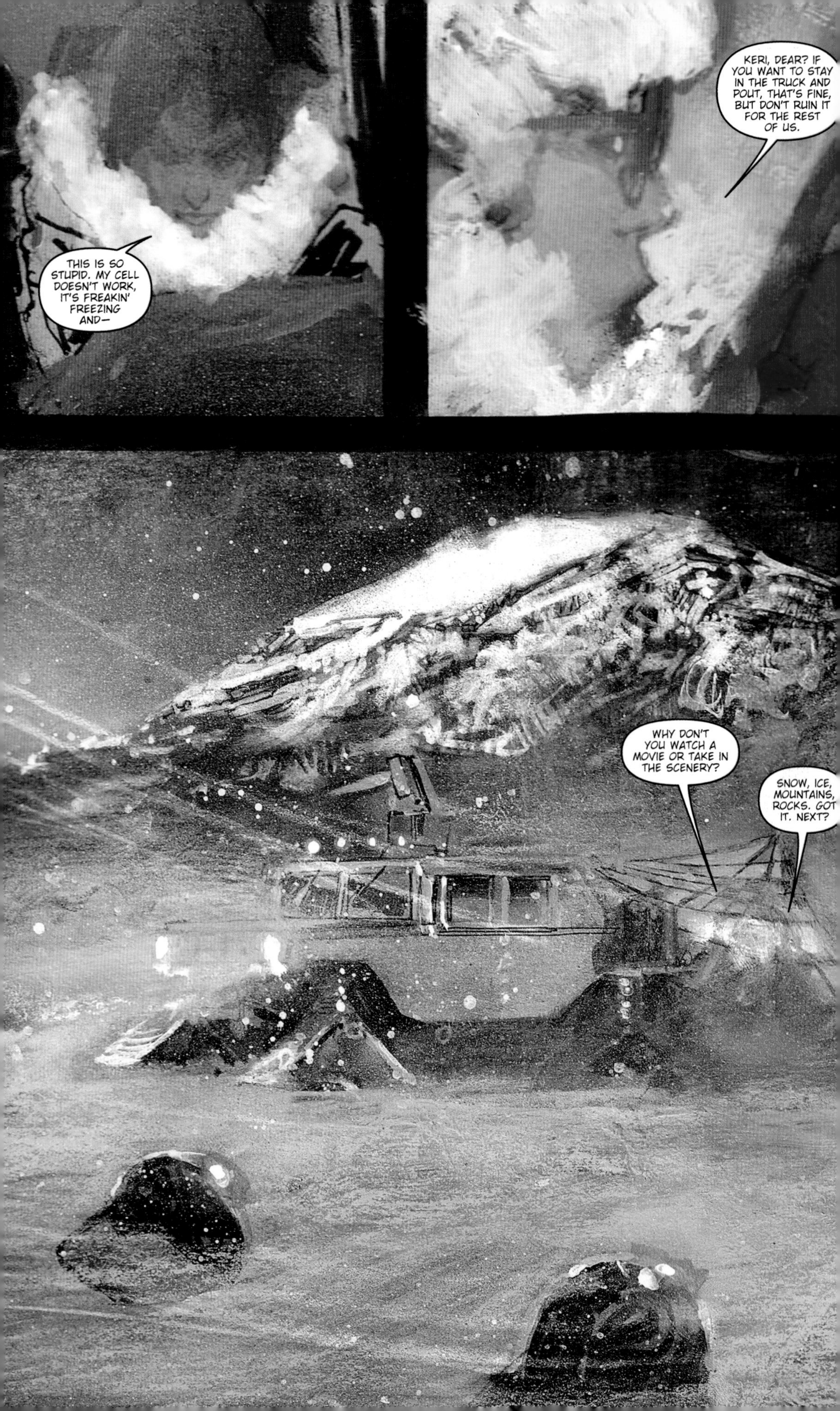
THIS IS SO STUPID. MY CELL DOESN'T WORK, IT'S FREAKIN' FREEZING AND—
KERI, DEAR? IF YOU WANT TO STAY IN THE TRUCK AND POUT, THAT'S FINE, BUT DON'T RUIN IT FOR THE REST OF US.
WHY DON'T YOU WATCH A MOVIE OR TAKE IN THE SCENERY?
SNOW, ICE, MOUNTAINS, ROCKS. GOT IT. NEXT?

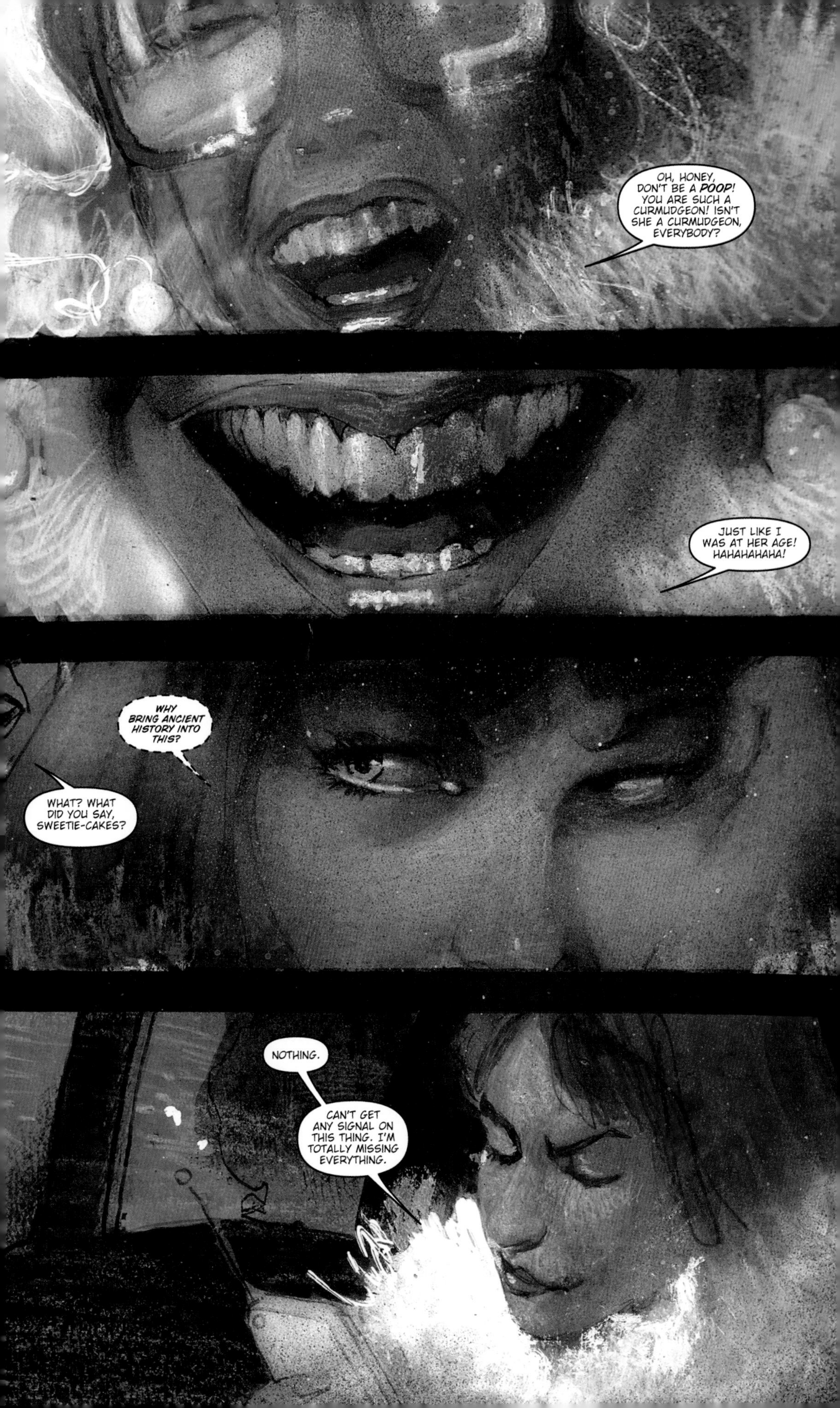
OH, HONEY, DON'T BE A POOP! YOU ARE SUCH A CURMUDGEON! ISN'T SHE A CURMUDGEON, EVERYBODY?
JUST LIKE I WAS AT HER AGE! HAHAHAHAHA!
WHY BRING ANCIENT HISTORY INTO THIS?
WHAT? WHAT DID YOU SAY, SWEETIE-CAKES?
NOTHING.
CAN'T GET ANY SIGNAL ON THIS THING. I'M TOTALLY MISSING EVERYTHING.

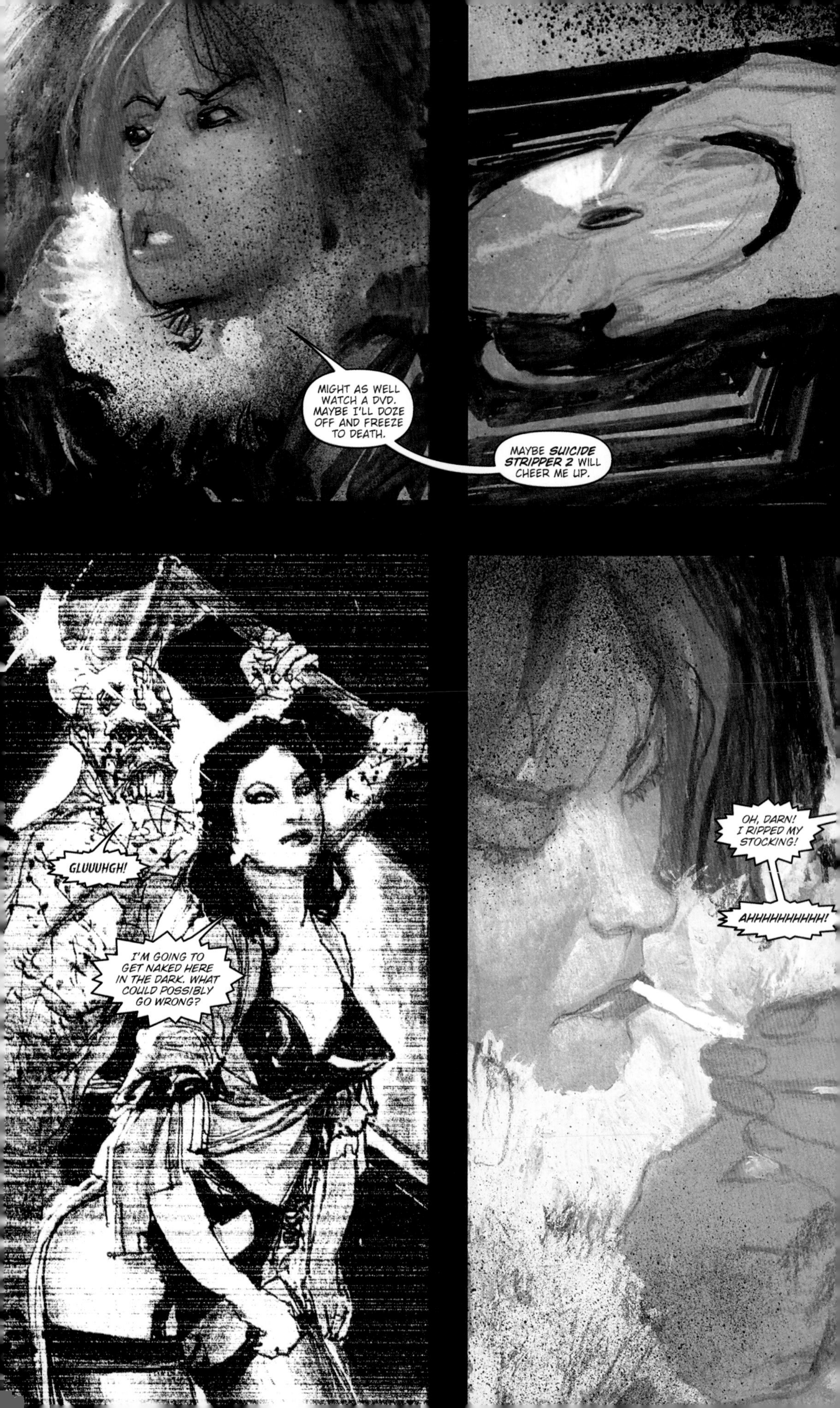

MIGHT AS WELL WATCH A DVD. MAYBE I'LL DOZE OFF AND FREEZE TO DEATH.
MAYBE SUICIDE STRIPPER 2 WILL CHEER ME UP.
GLUUUHGH!
I'M GOING TO GET NAKED HERE IN THE DARK. WHAT COULD POSSIBLY GO WRONG?
OH, DARN! I RIPPED MY STOCKING!
AHHHHHHHHHHH!

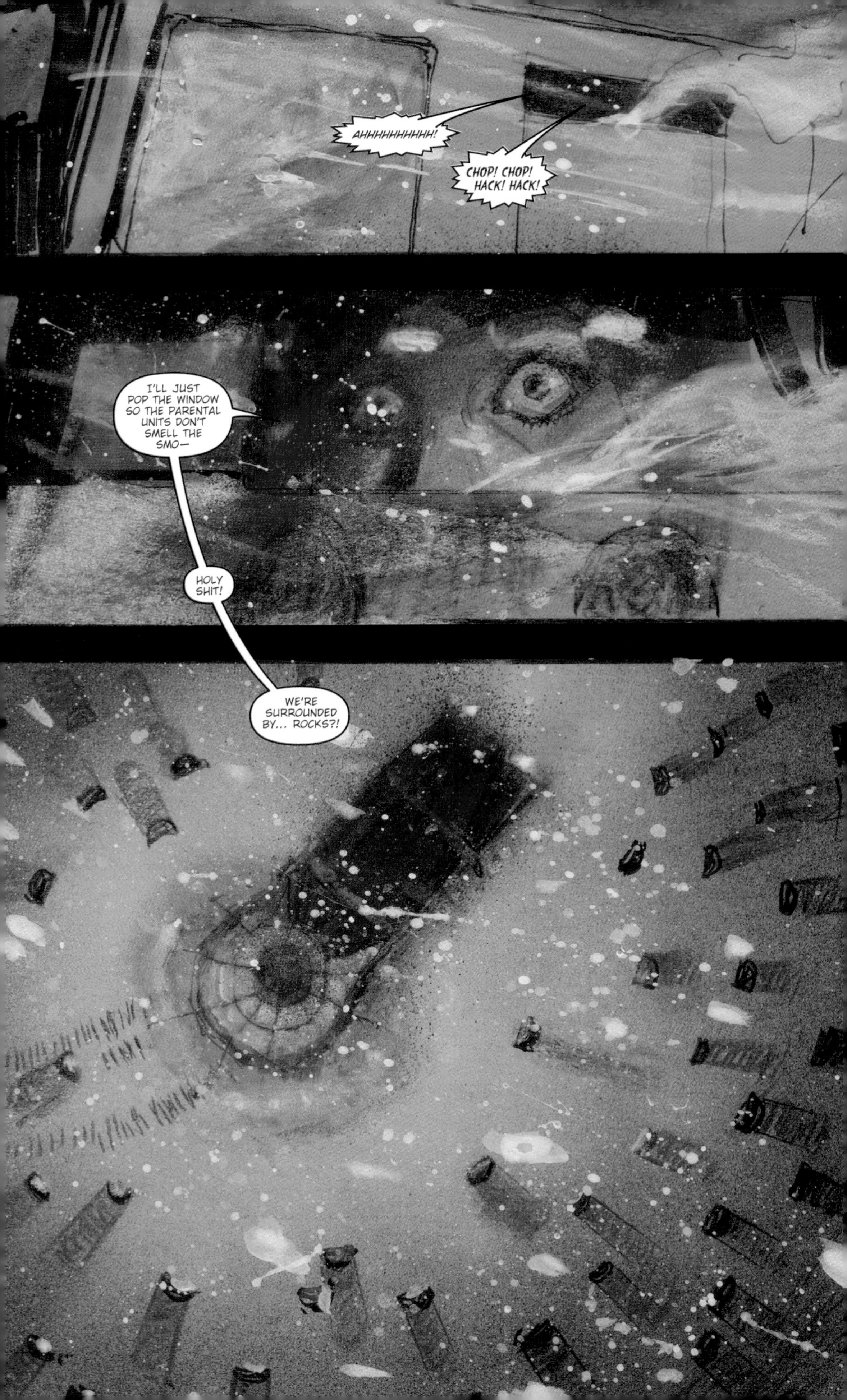
AHHHHHHHHHHH!
CHOP! CHOP! HACK! HACK!
I'LL JUST POP THE WINDOW SO THE PARENTAL UNITS DON'T SMELL THE SMO—
HOLY SHIT!
WE'RE SURROUNDED BY... ROCKS?!

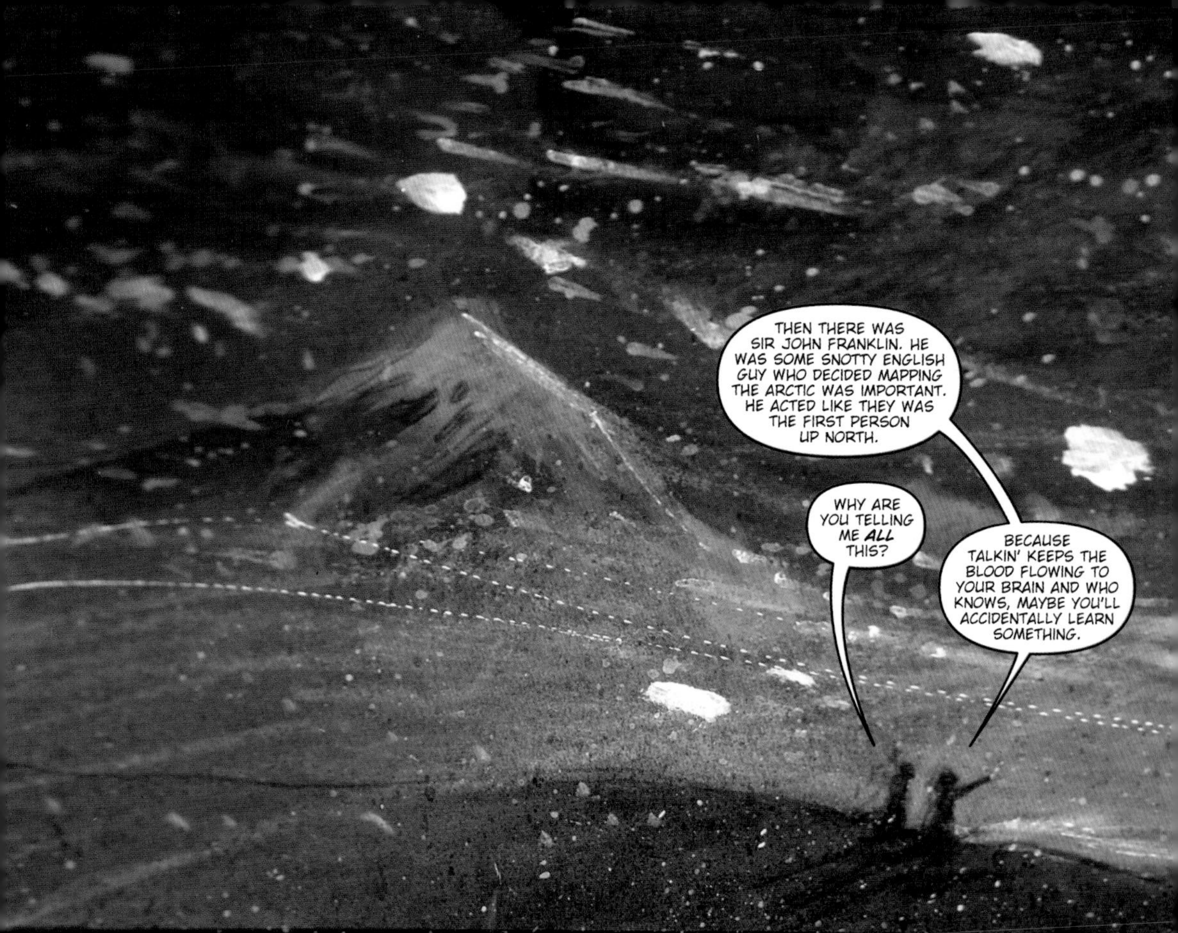
THEN THERE WAS SIR JOHN FRANKLIN. HE WAS SOME SNOTTY ENGLISH GUY WHO DECIDED MAPPING THE ARCTIC WAS IMPORTANT. HE ACTED LIKE THEY WAS THE FIRST PERSON UP NORTH.
WHY ARE YOU TELLING ME ALL THIS?
BECAUSE TALKIN' KEEPS THE BLOOD FLOWING TO YOUR BRAIN AND WHO KNOWS, MAYBE YOU'LL ACCIDENTALLY LEARN SOMETHING.

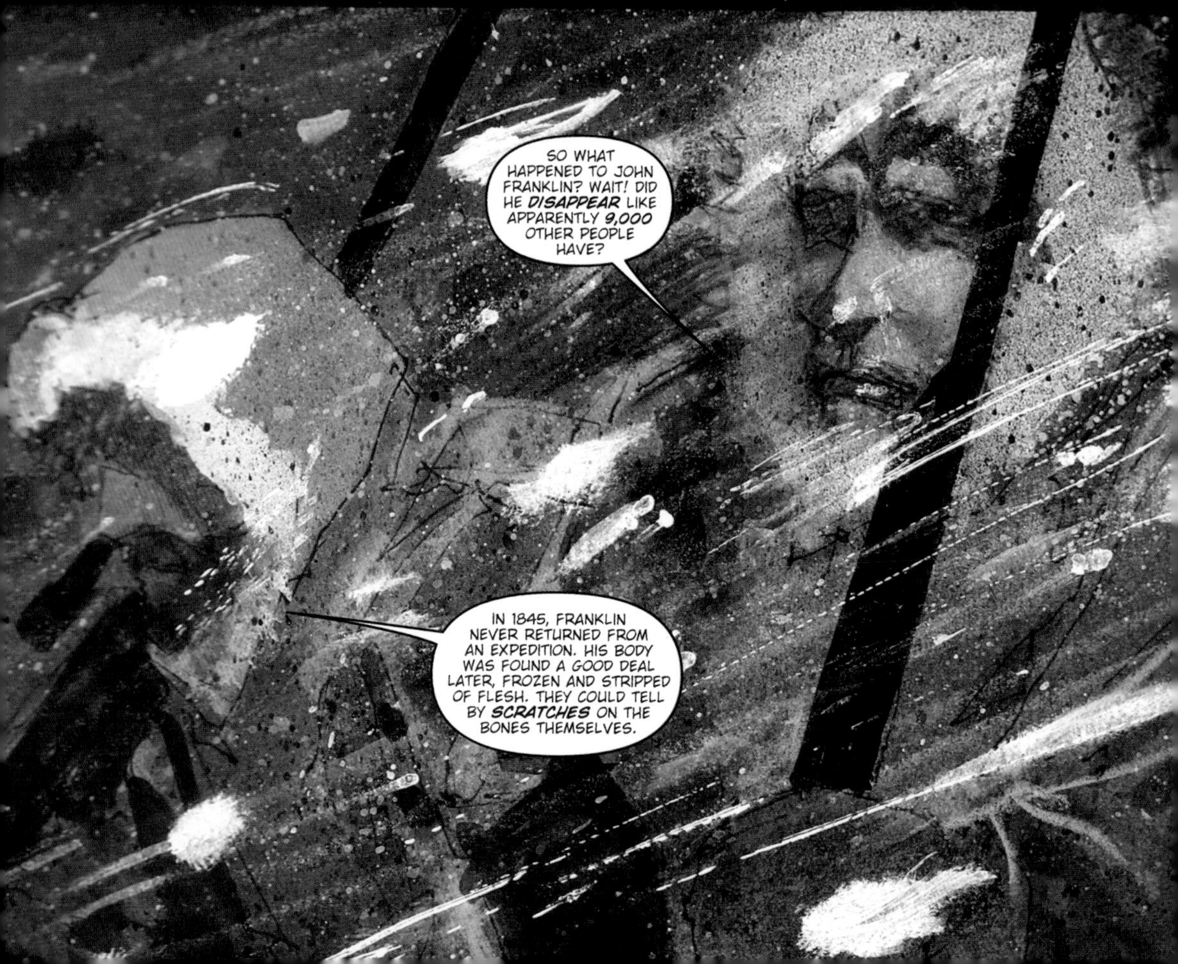
SO WHAT HAPPENED TO JOHN FRANKLIN? WAIT! DID HE DISAPPEAR LIKE APPARENTLY 9,000 OTHER PEOPLE HAVE?
IN 1845, FRANKLIN NEVER RETURNED FROM AN EXPEDITION. HIS BODY WAS FOUND A GOOD DEAL LATER, FROZEN AND STRIPPED OF FLESH. THEY COULD TELL BY SCRATCHES ON THE BONES THEMSELVES.

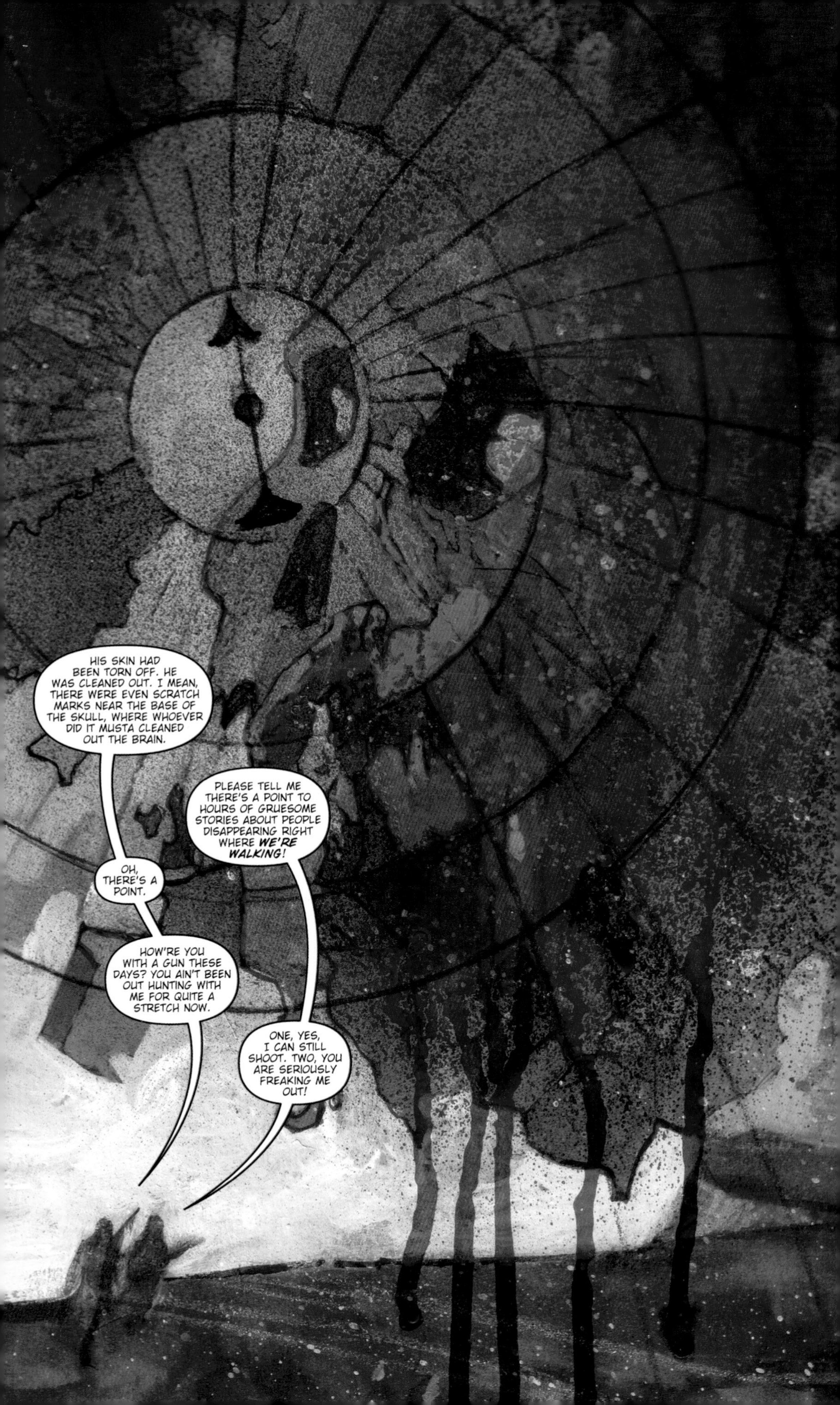

HIS SKIN HAD BEEN TORN OFF. HE WAS CLEANED OUT. I MEAN, THERE WERE EVEN SCRATCH MARKS NEAR THE BASE OF THE SKULL, WHERE WHOEVER DID IT MUSTA CLEANED OUT THE BRAIN.
PLEASE TELL ME THERE'S A POINT TO HOURS OF GRUESOME STORIES ABOUT PEOPLE DISAPPEARING RIGHT WHERE **WE'RE WALKING**!
OH, THERE'S A POINT.
HOW'RE YOU WITH A GUN THESE DAYS? YOU AIN'T BEEN OUT HUNTING WITH ME FOR QUITE A STRETCH NOW.
ONE, YES, I CAN STILL SHOOT. TWO, YOU ARE SERIOUSLY FREAKING ME OUT!

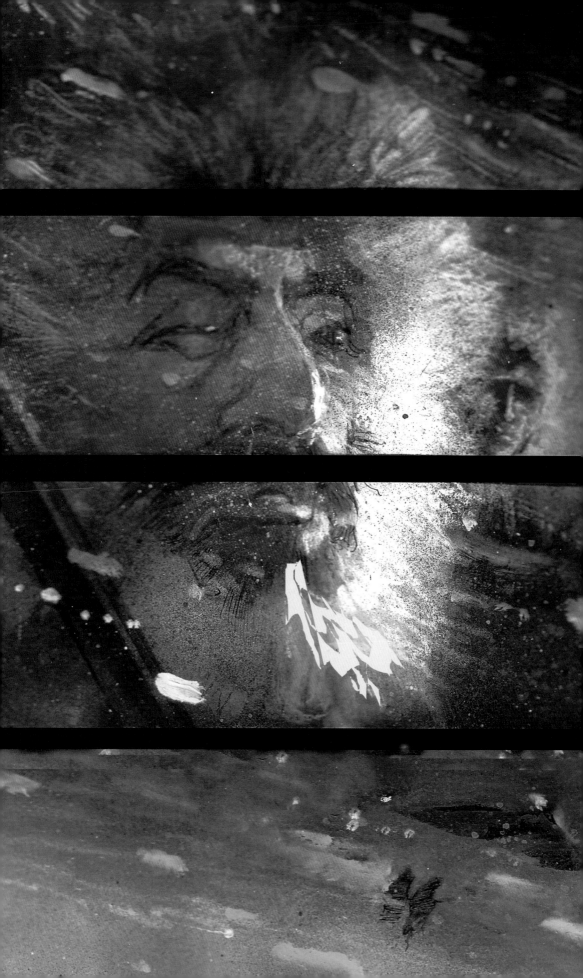

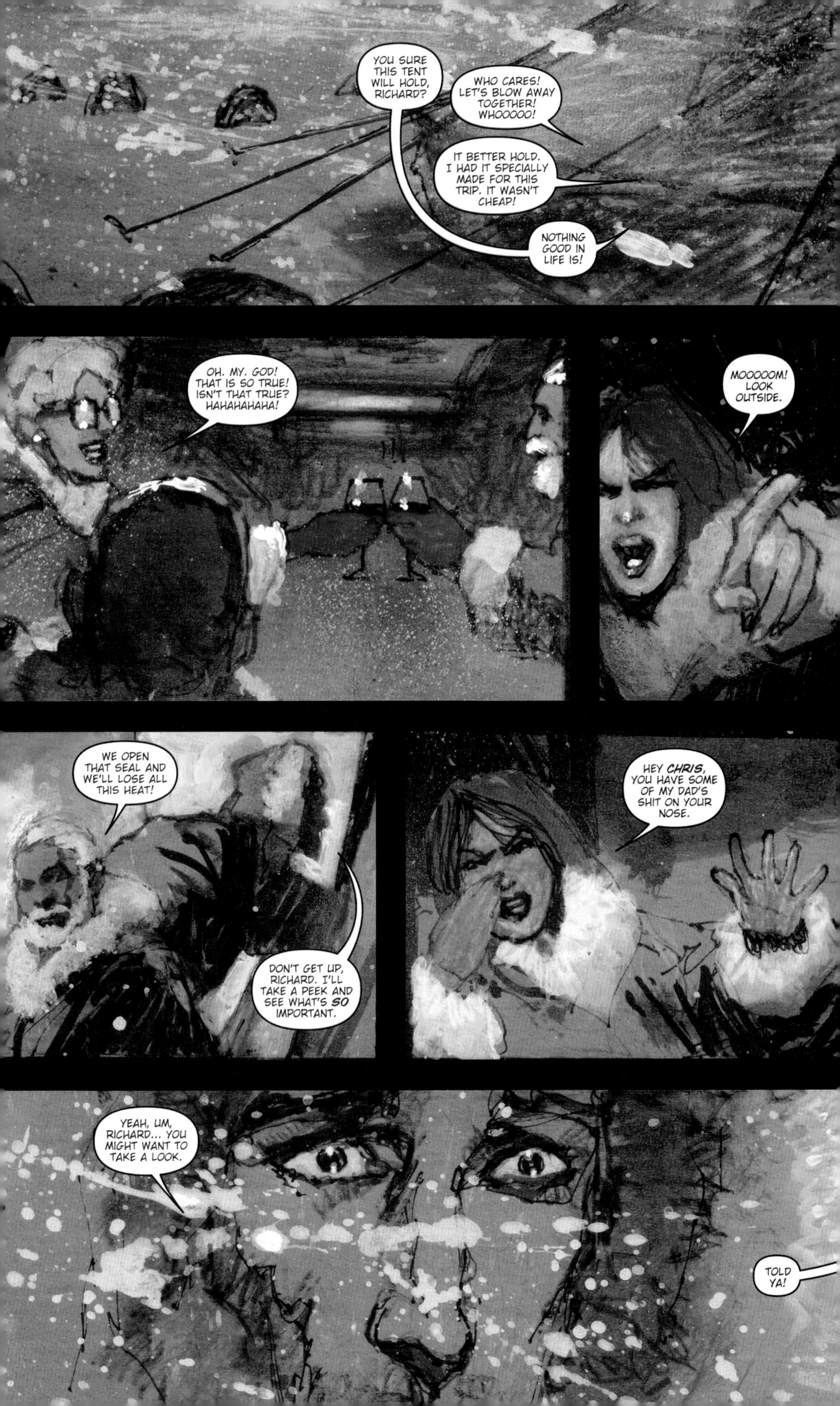
YOU SURE THIS TENT WILL HOLD, RICHARD?
WHO CARES! LET'S BLOW AWAY TOGETHER! WHOOOOO!
IT BETTER HOLD. I HAD IT SPECIALLY MADE FOR THIS TRIP. IT WASN'T CHEAP!
NOTHING GOOD IN LIFE IS!
OH. MY. GOD! THAT IS SO TRUE! ISN'T THAT TRUE? HAHAHAHAHA!
MOOOOOM! LOOK OUTSIDE.
WE OPEN THAT SEAL AND WE'LL LOSE ALL THIS HEAT!
DON'T GET UP, RICHARD. I'LL TAKE A PEEK AND SEE WHAT'S SO IMPORTANT.
HEY CHRIS, YOU HAVE SOME OF MY DAD'S SHIT ON YOUR NOSE.
YEAH, UM, RICHARD... YOU MIGHT WANT TO TAKE A LOOK.
TOLD YA!

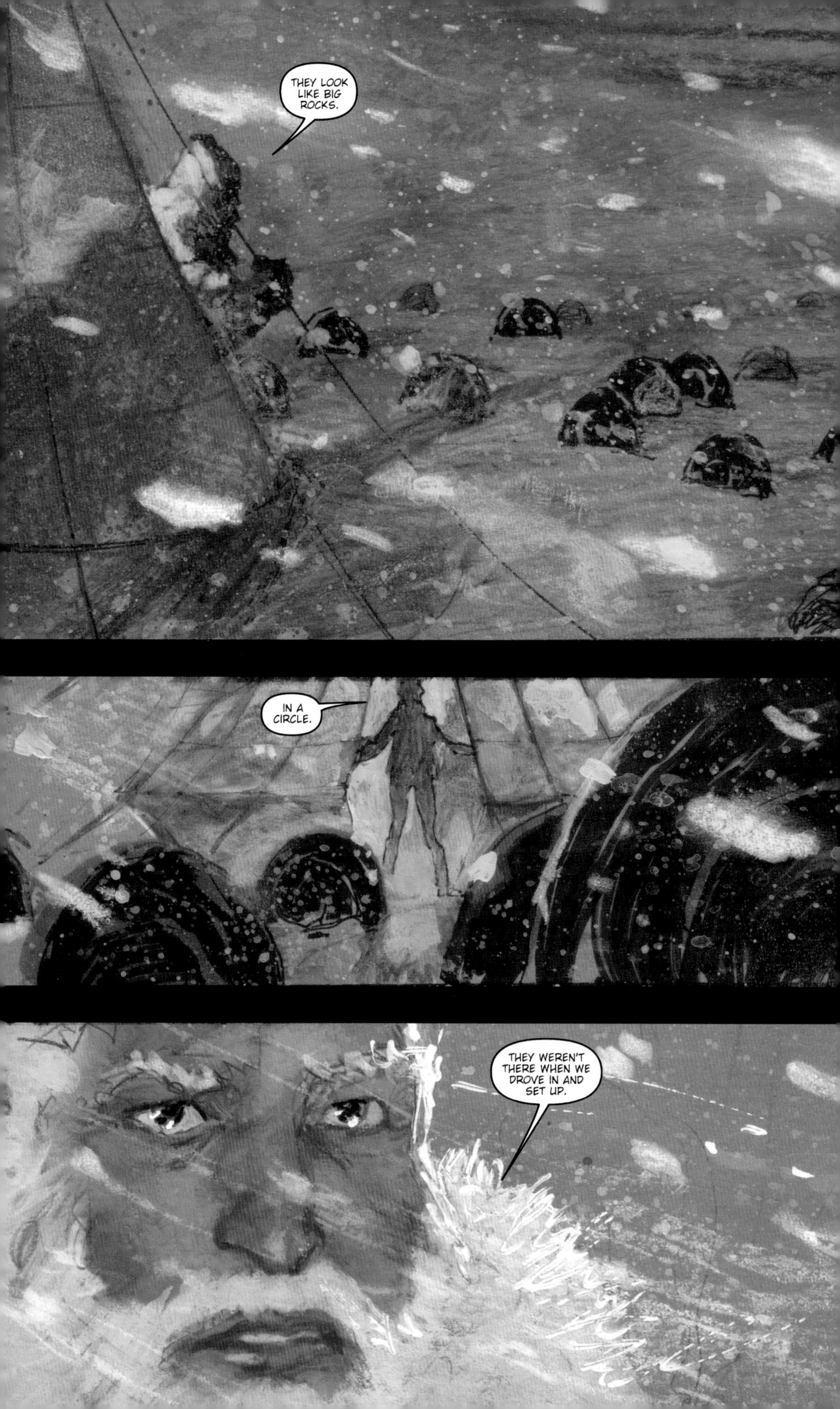
THEY LOOK LIKE BIG ROCKS.
IN A CIRCLE.
THEY WEREN'T THERE WHEN WE DROVE IN AND SET UP.

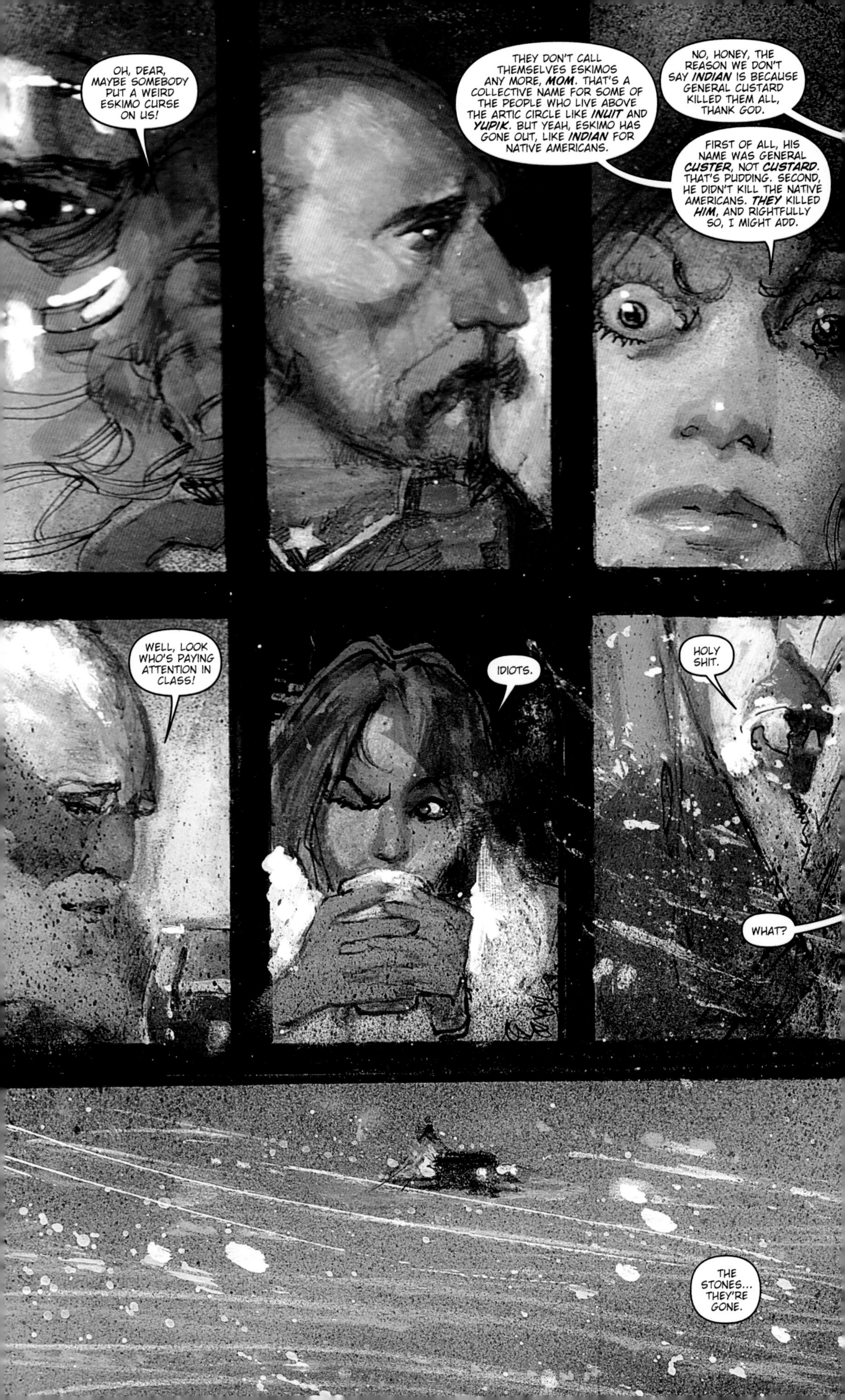
OH, DEAR, MAYBE SOMEBODY PUT A WEIRD ESKIMO CURSE ON US!
THEY DON'T CALL THEMSELVES ESKIMOS ANY MORE, MOM. THAT'S A COLLECTIVE NAME FOR SOME OF THE PEOPLE WHO LIVE ABOVE THE ARTIC CIRCLE LIKE INUIT AND YUPIK. BUT YEAH, ESKIMO HAS GONE OUT, LIKE INDIAN FOR NATIVE AMERICANS.
NO, HONEY, THE REASON WE DON'T SAY INDIAN IS BECAUSE GENERAL CUSTARD KILLED THEM ALL, THANK GOD.
FIRST OF ALL, HIS NAME WAS GENERAL CUSTER, NOT CUSTARD. THAT'S PUDDING. SECOND, HE DIDN'T KILL THE NATIVE AMERICANS. THEY KILLED HIM, AND RIGHTFULLY SO, I MIGHT ADD.
WELL, LOOK WHO'S PAYING ATTENTION IN CLASS!
IDIOTS.
HOLY SHIT.
WHAT?
THE STONES... THEY'RE GONE.

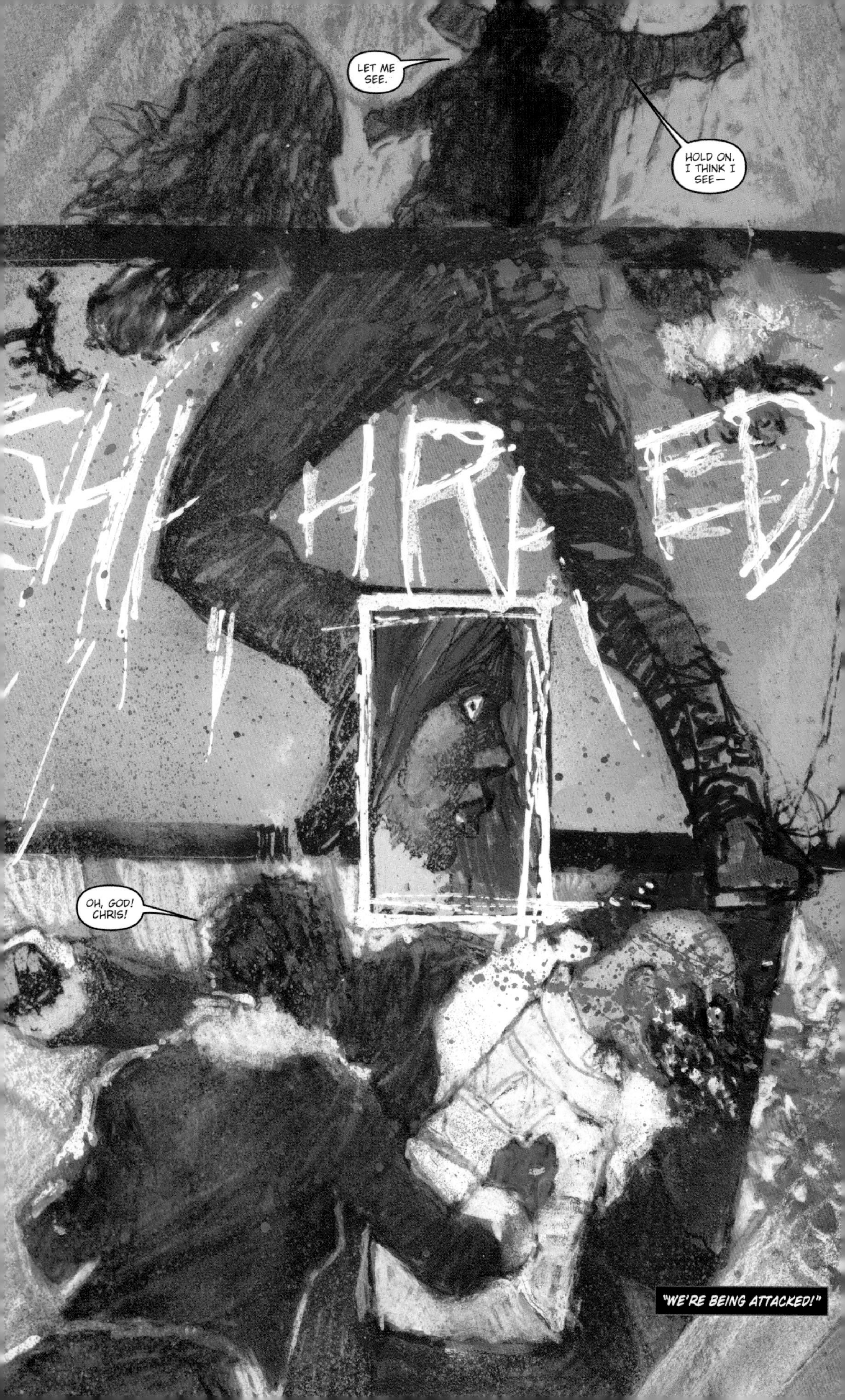
LET ME SEE.
HOLD ON. I THINK I SEE—
OH, GOD! CHRIS!
"WE'RE BEING ATTACKED!"

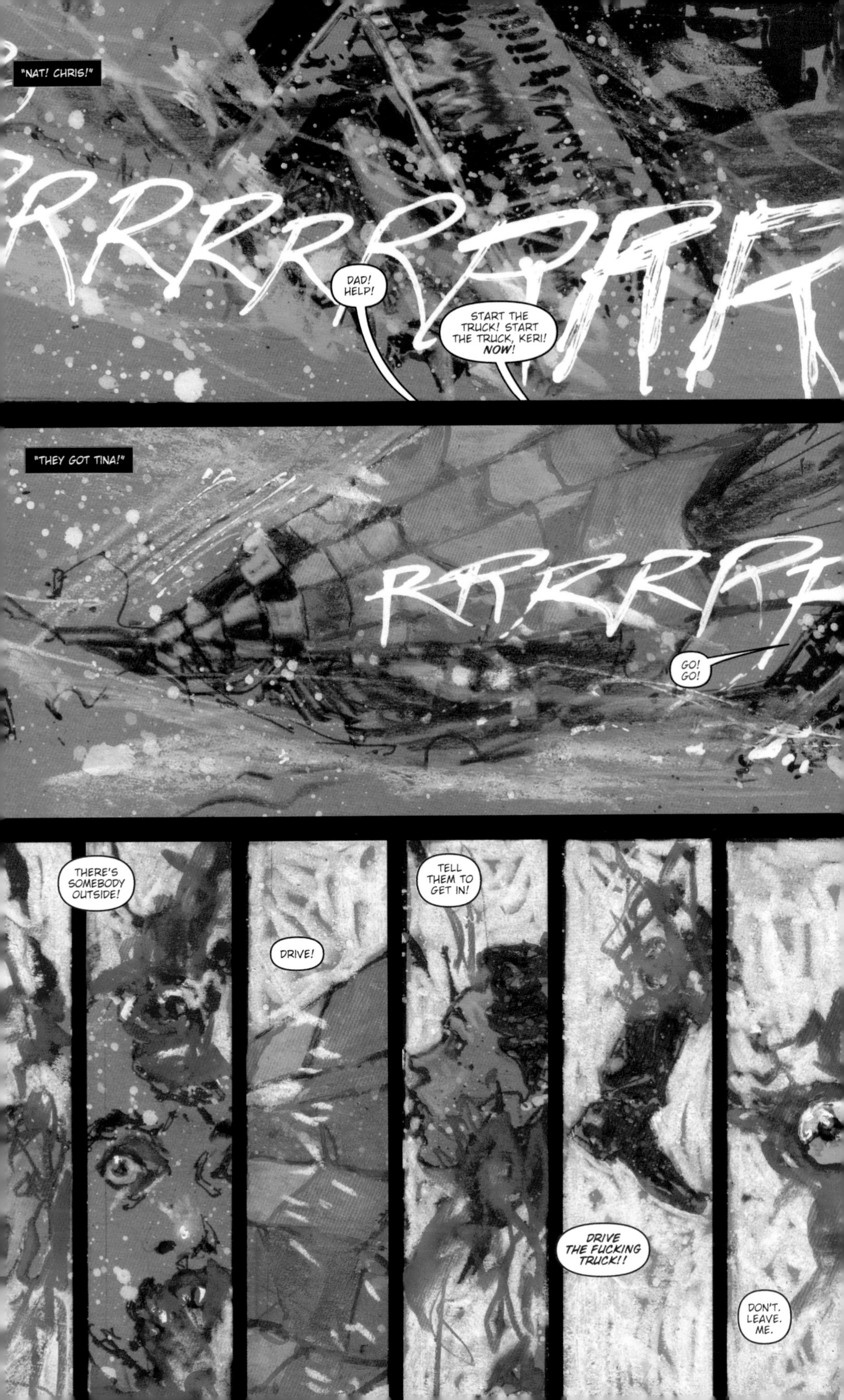
"NAT! CHRIS!"
RRRRRRAAAA
DAD! HELP!
START THE TRUCK! START THE TRUCK, KERI! NOW!
"THEY GOT TINA!"
RRRRRAA
GO! GO!
THERE'S SOMEBODY OUTSIDE!
DRIVE!
TELL THEM TO GET IN!
DRIVE THE FUCKING TRUCK!!
DON'T. LEAVE. ME.

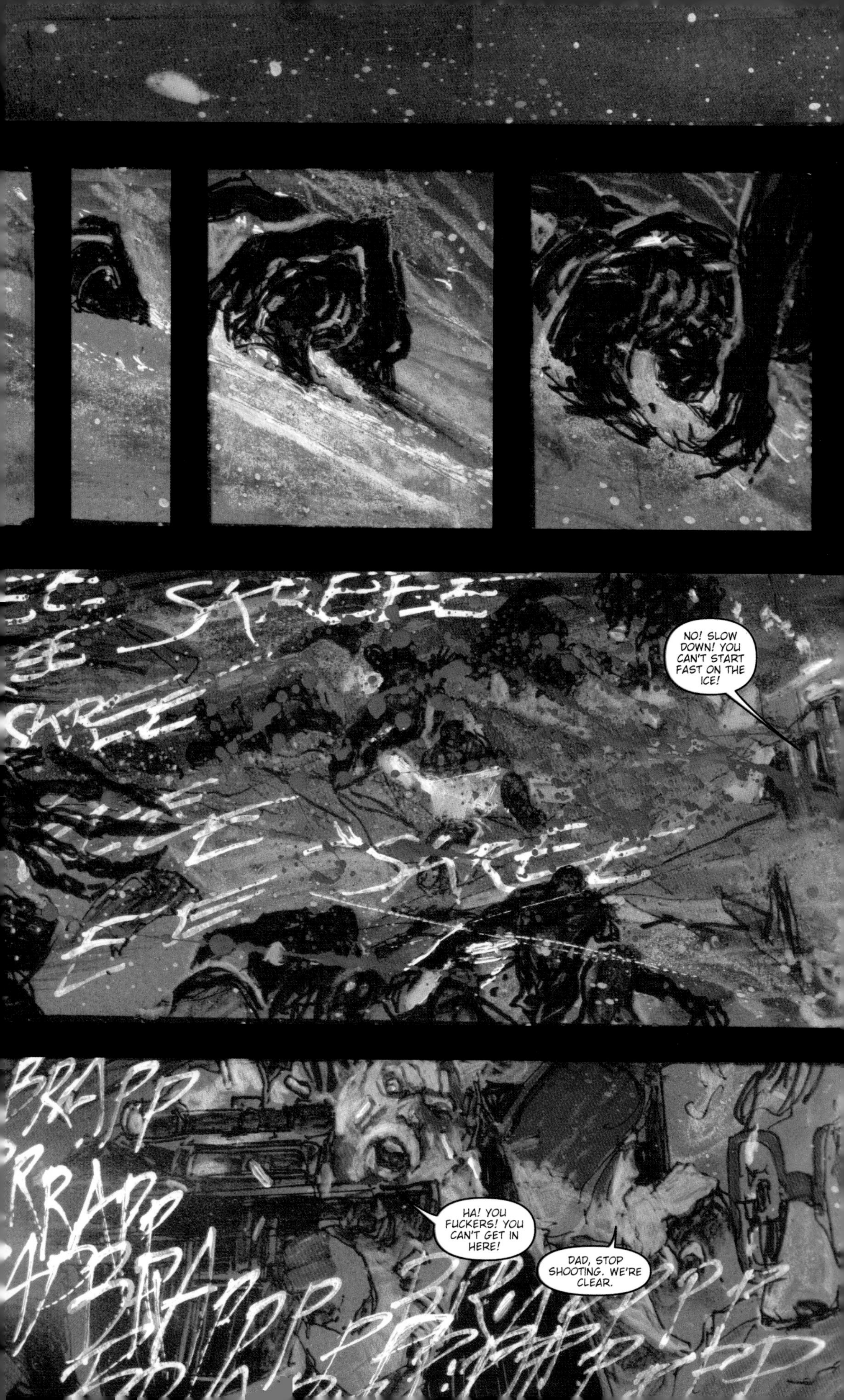
NO! SLOW DOWN! YOU CAN'T START FAST ON THE ICE!
HA! YOU FUCKERS! YOU CAN'T GET IN HERE!
DAD, STOP SHOOTING. WE'RE CLEAR.

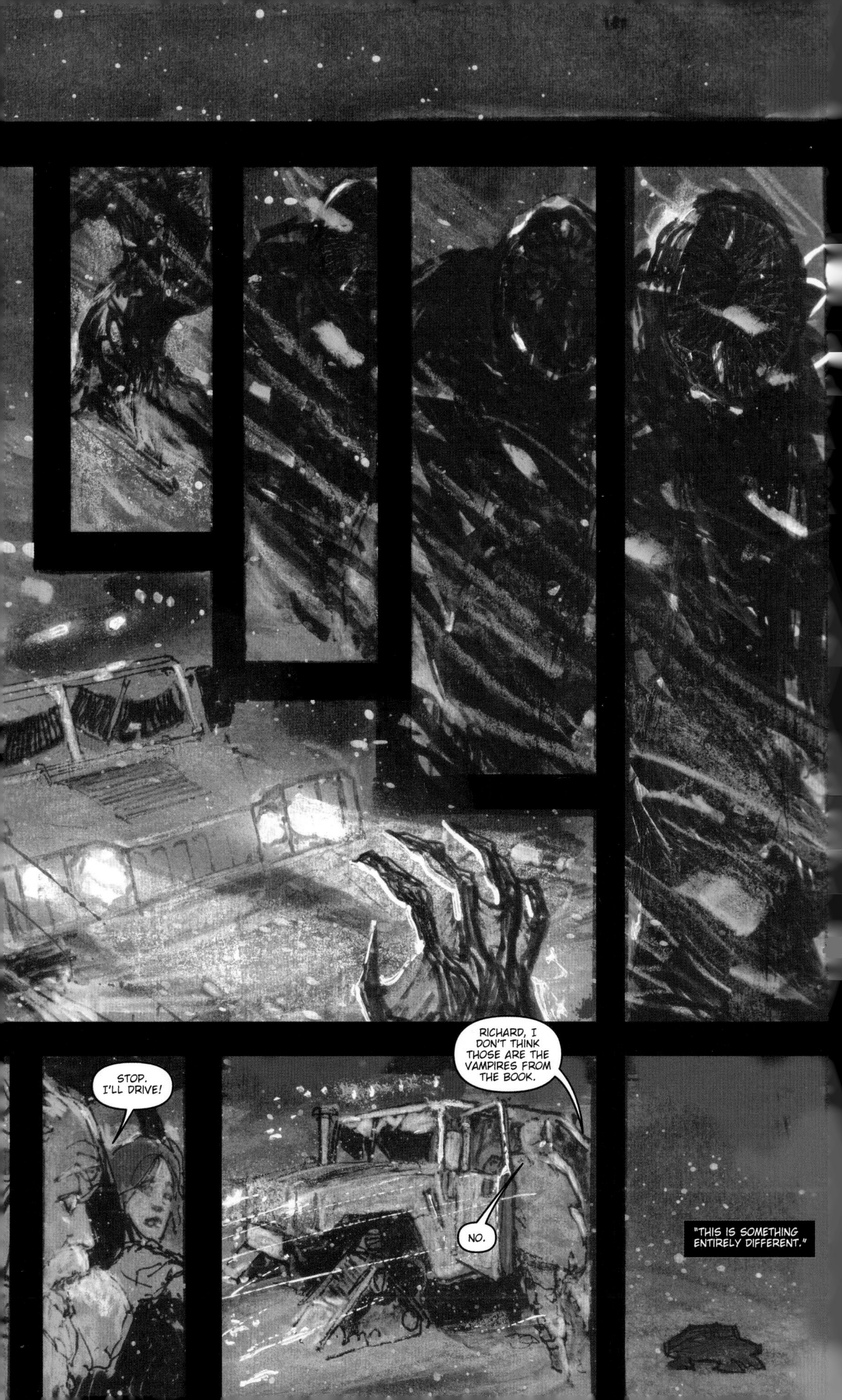
STOP. I'LL DRIVE!
RICHARD, I DON'T THINK THOSE ARE THE VAMPIRES FROM THE BOOK.
NO.
"THIS IS SOMETHING ENTIRELY DIFFERENT."

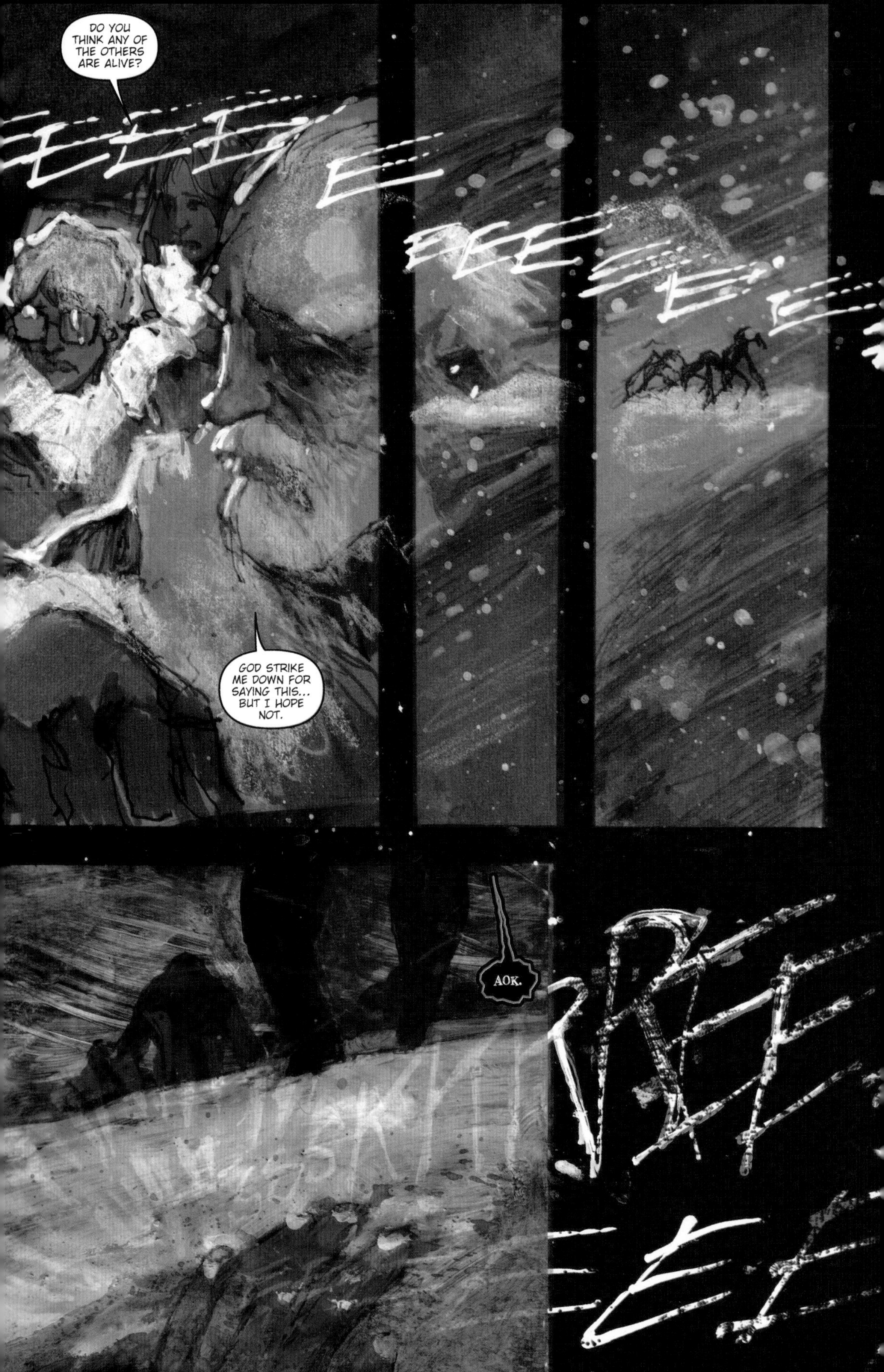
DO YOU THINK ANY OF THE OTHERS ARE ALIVE?
GOD STRIKE ME DOWN FOR SAYING THIS... BUT I HOPE NOT.
AOK.

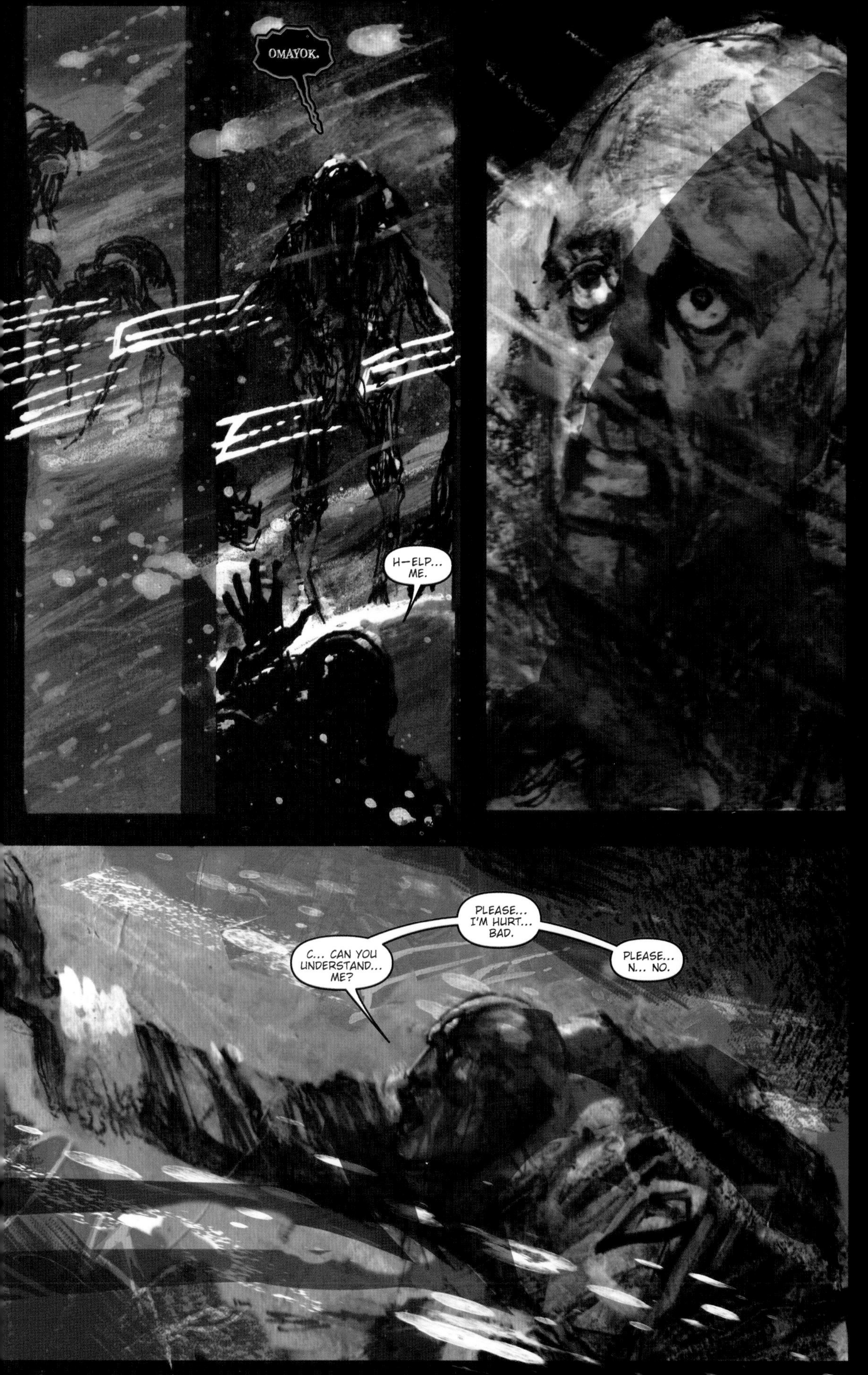
OMAYOK.
H—ELP... ME.
C... CAN YOU UNDERSTAND... ME?
PLEASE... I'M HURT... BAD.
PLEASE... N... NO.

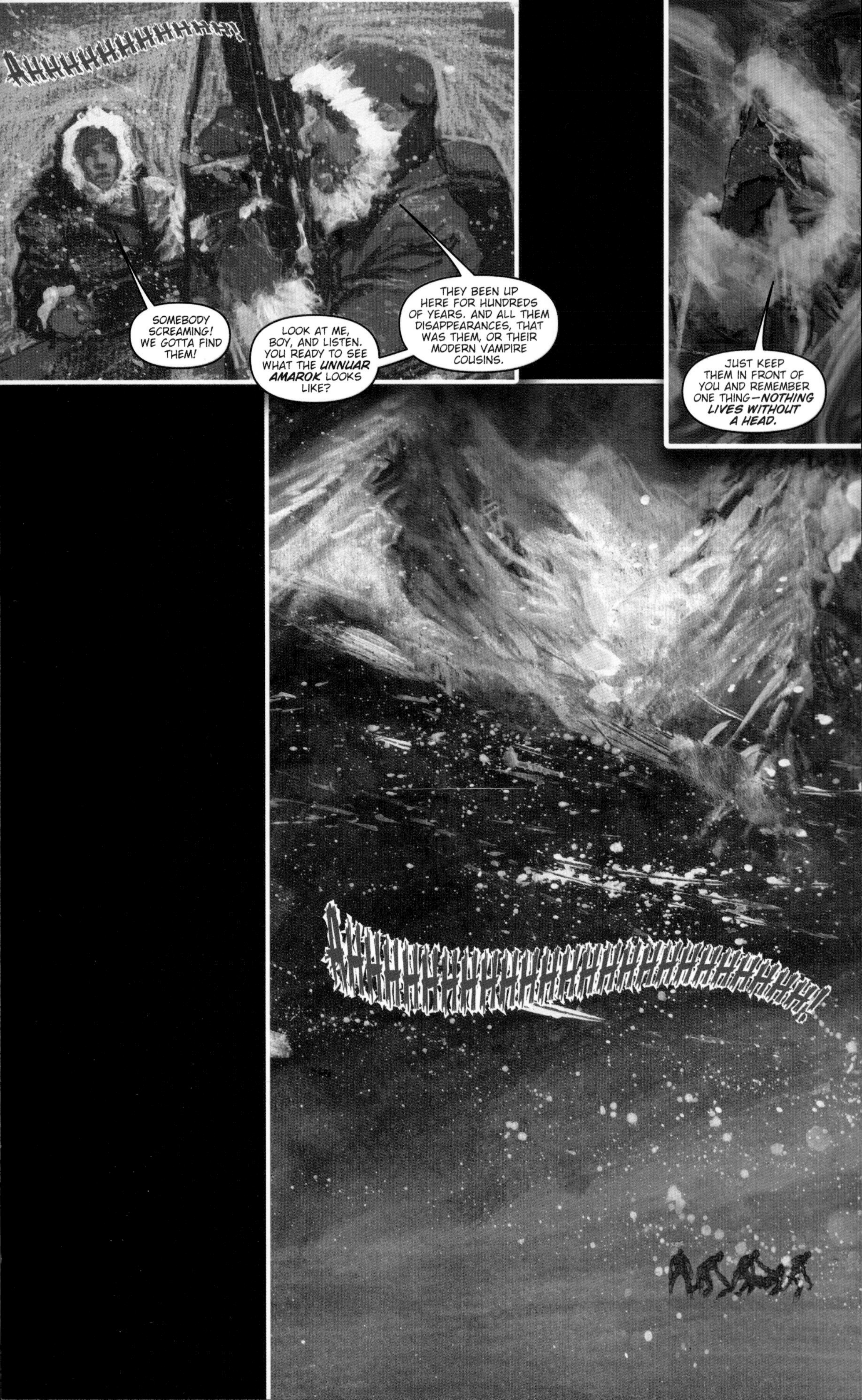
AHHHHHHHHHHHHHH!
SOMEBODY SCREAMING! WE GOTTA FIND THEM!
LOOK AT ME, BOY, AND LISTEN. YOU READY TO SEE WHAT THE ***UNNUAR AMAROK*** LOOKS LIKE?
THEY BEEN UP HERE FOR HUNDREDS OF YEARS. AND ALL THEM DISAPPEARANCES, THAT WAS THEM, OR THEIR MODERN VAMPIRE COUSINS.
JUST KEEP THEM IN FRONT OF YOU AND REMEMBER ONE THING—***NOTHING LIVES WITHOUT A HEAD.***
AHHHHHHHHHHHHHHHHHHHHHHHHHHHHHH!

chapter three

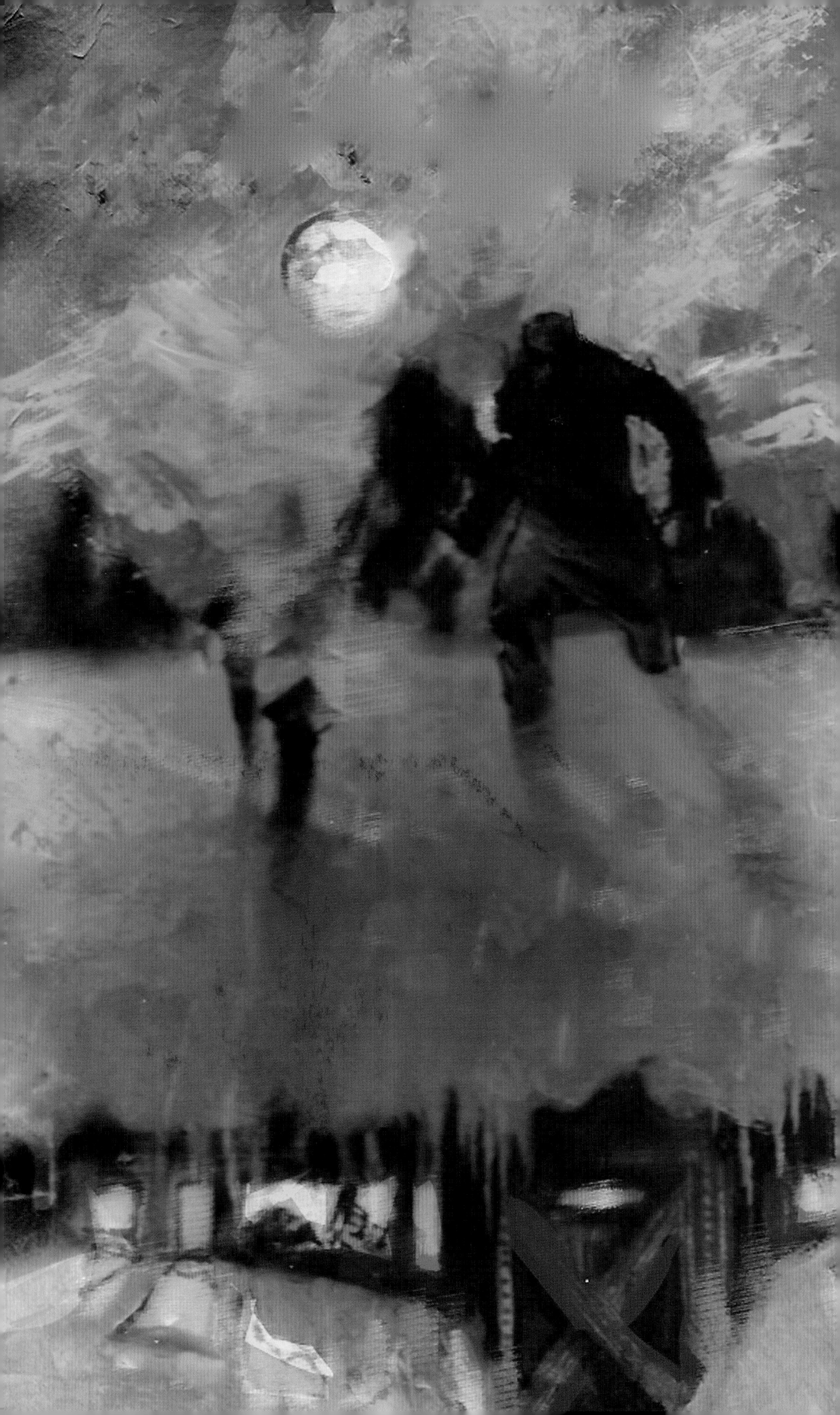

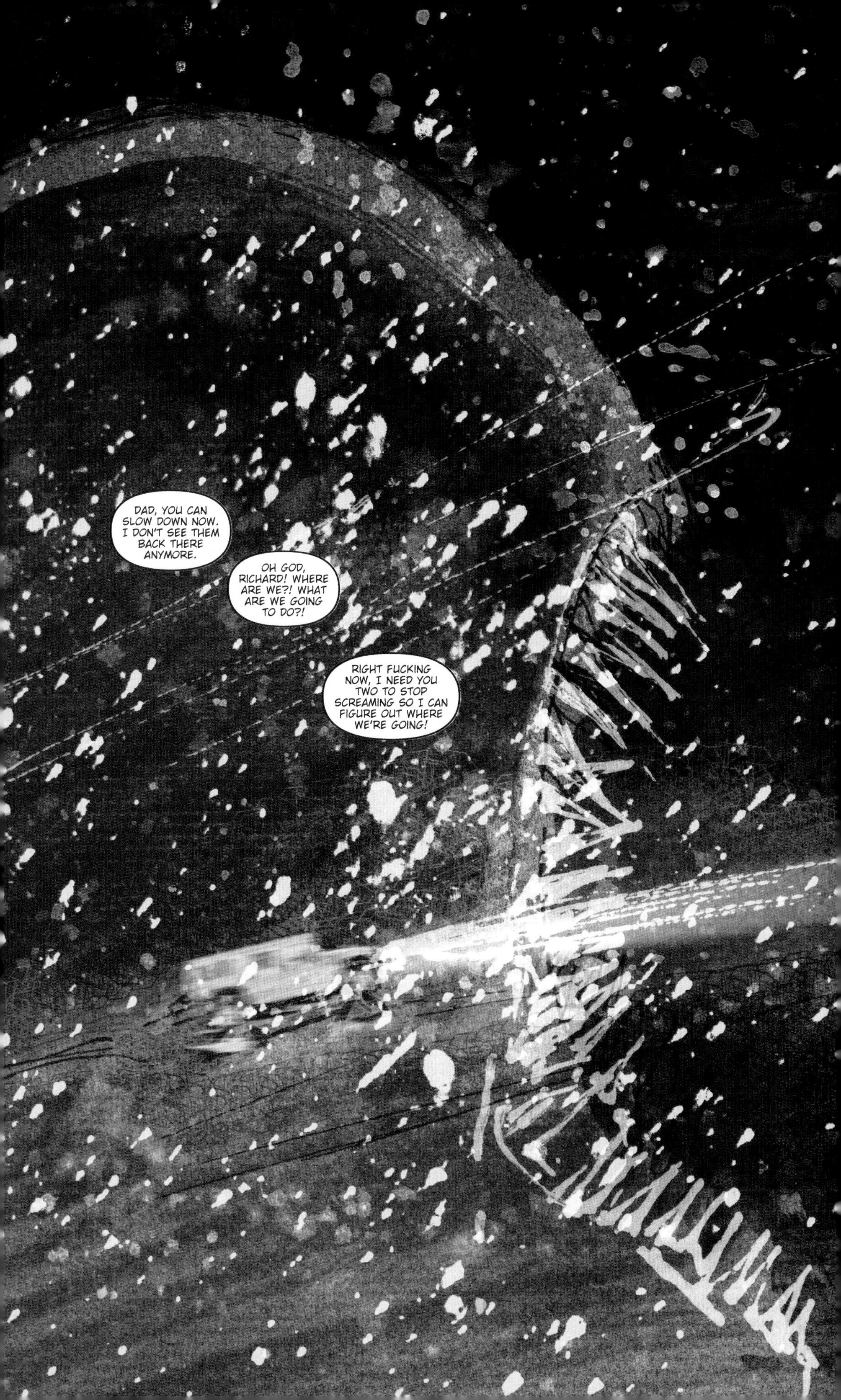
DAD, YOU CAN SLOW DOWN NOW. I DON'T SEE THEM BACK THERE ANYMORE.
OH GOD, RICHARD! WHERE ARE WE?! WHAT ARE WE GOING TO DO?!
RIGHT FUCKING NOW, I NEED YOU TWO TO STOP SCREAMING SO I CAN FIGURE OUT WHERE WE'RE GOING!

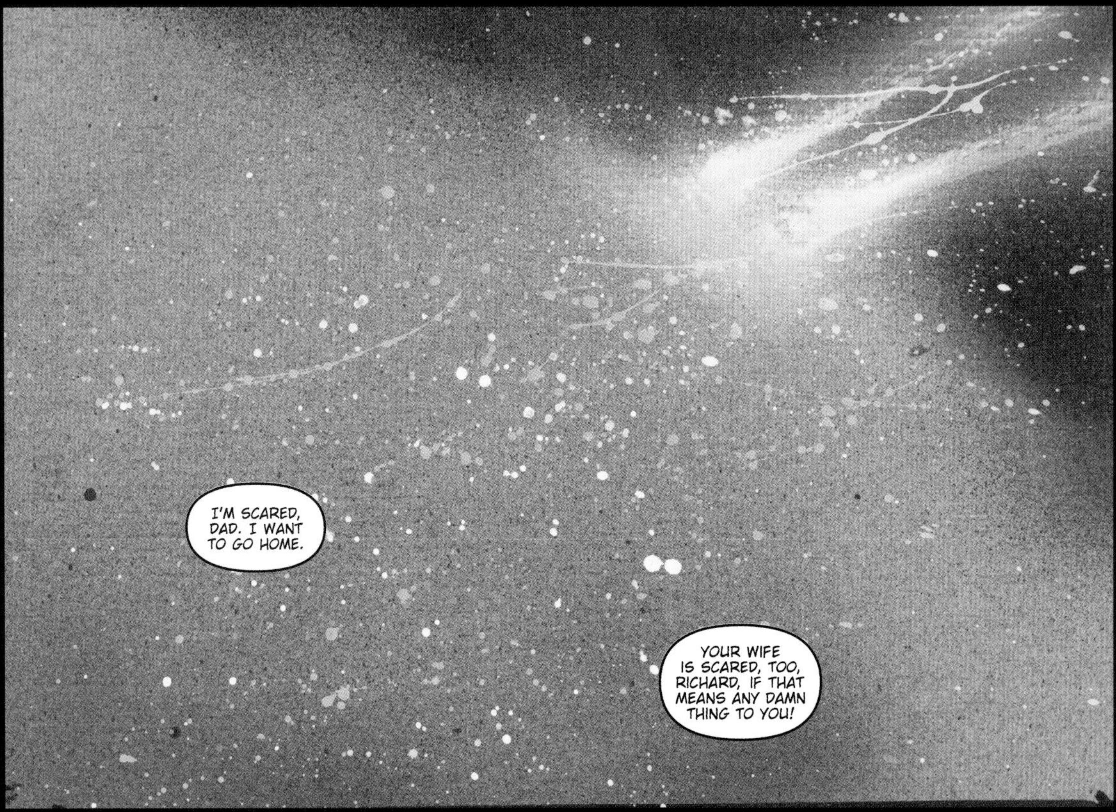
I'M SCARED, DAD. I WANT TO GO HOME.
YOUR WIFE IS SCARED, TOO, RICHARD, IF THAT MEANS ANY DAMN THING TO YOU!

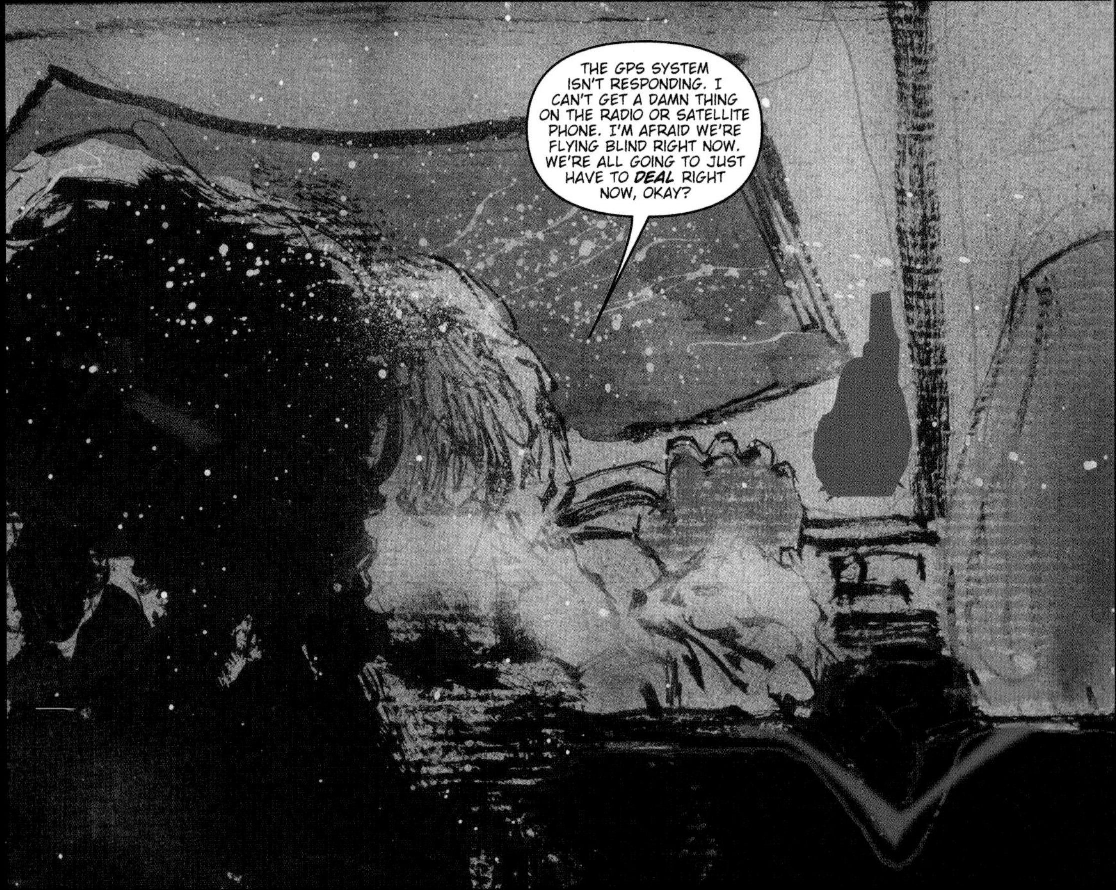
THE GPS SYSTEM ISN'T RESPONDING. I CAN'T GET A DAMN THING ON THE RADIO OR SATELLITE PHONE. I'M AFRAID WE'RE FLYING BLIND RIGHT NOW. WE'RE ALL GOING TO JUST HAVE TO **DEAL** RIGHT NOW, OKAY?

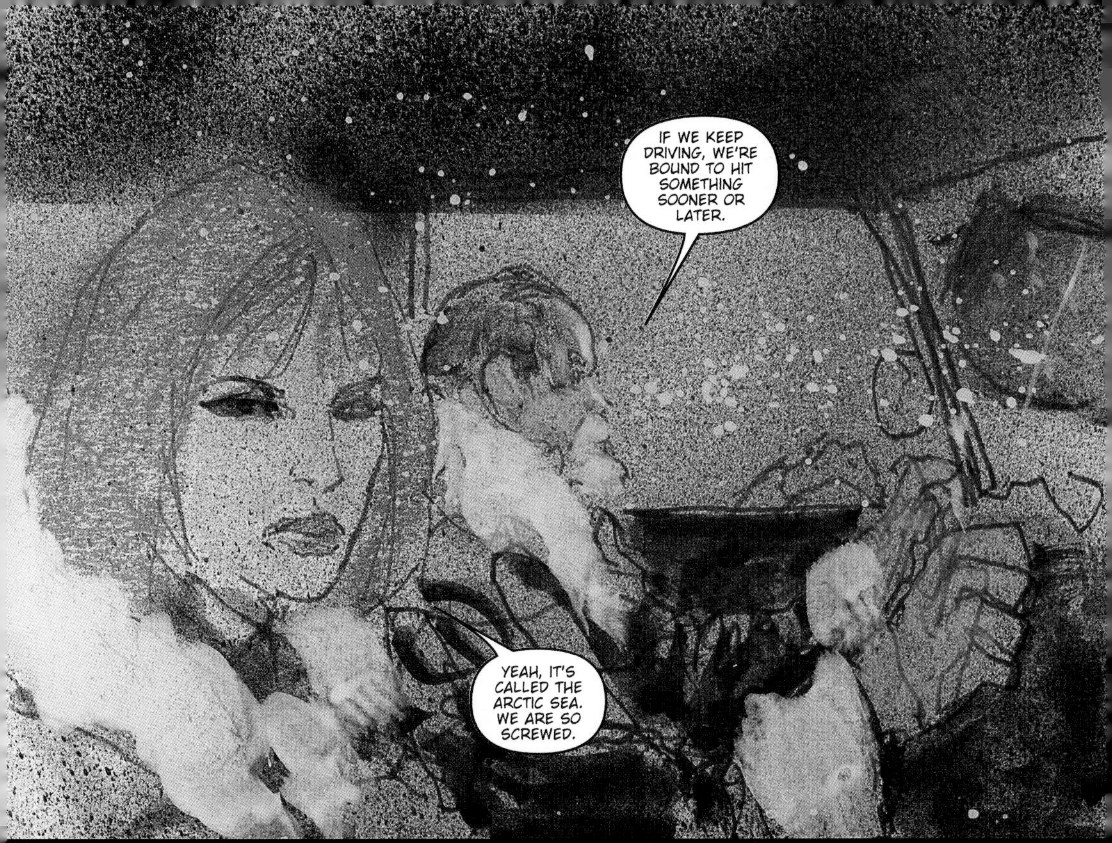
IF WE KEEP DRIVING, WE'RE BOUND TO HIT SOMETHING SOONER OR LATER.
YEAH, IT'S CALLED THE ARCTIC SEA. WE ARE SO SCREWED.

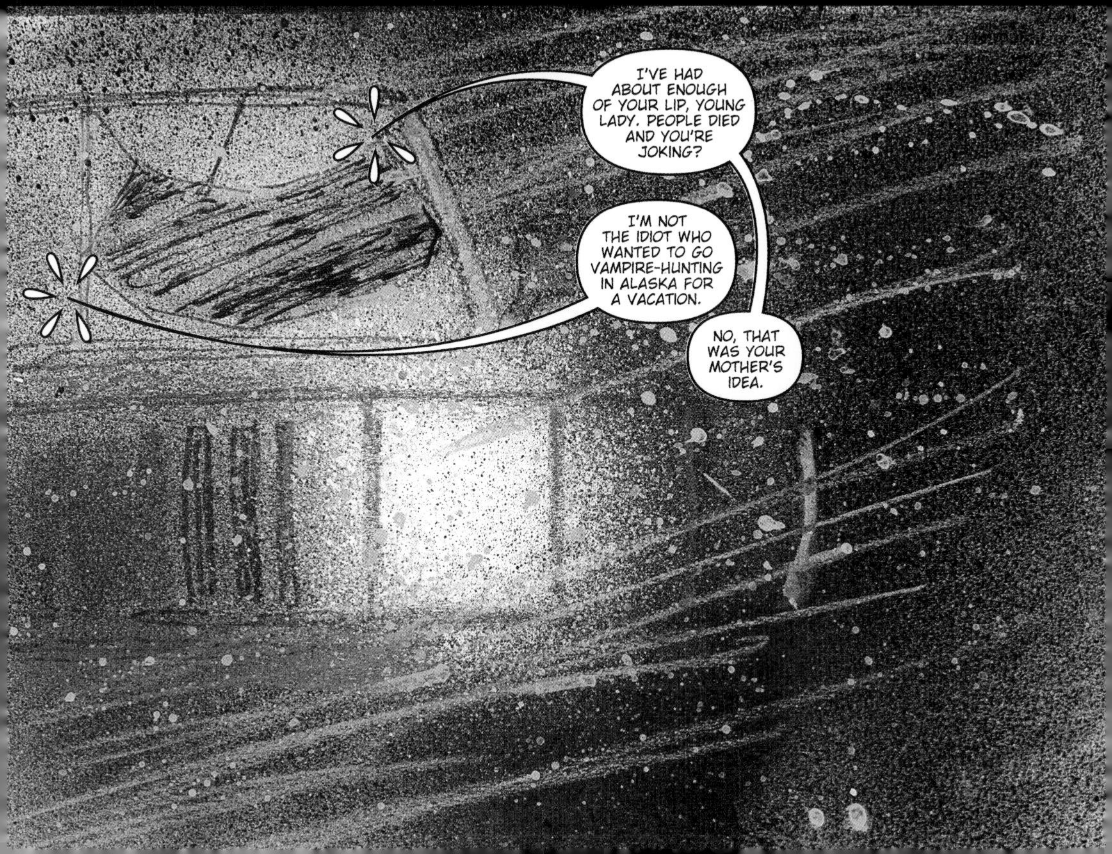
I'VE HAD ABOUT ENOUGH OF YOUR LIP, YOUNG LADY. PEOPLE DIED AND YOU'RE JOKING?
I'M NOT THE IDIOT WHO WANTED TO GO VAMPIRE-HUNTING IN ALASKA FOR A VACATION.
NO, THAT WAS YOUR MOTHER'S IDEA.

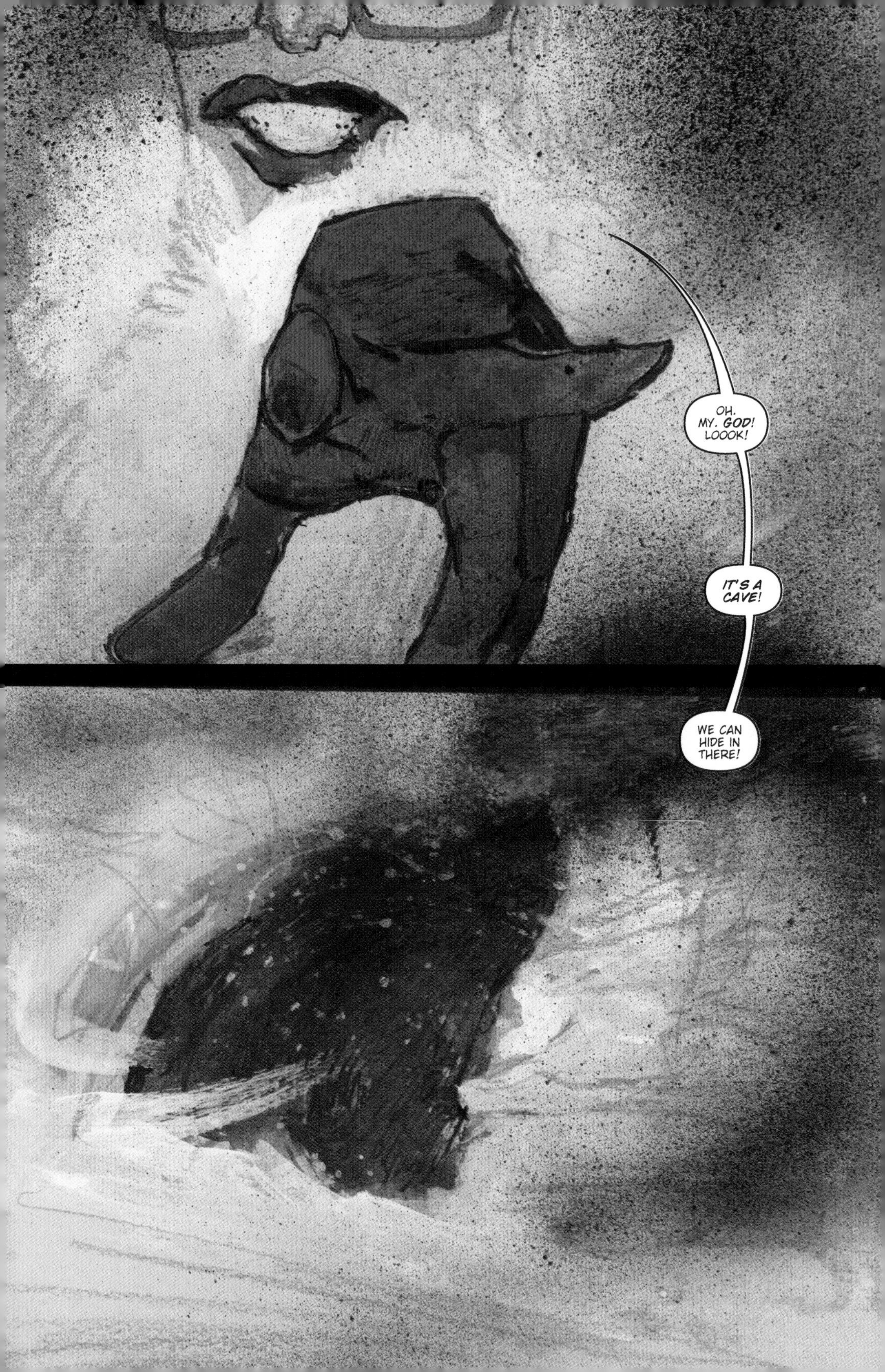
OH. MY. GOD! LOOOK!
IT'S A CAVE!
WE CAN HIDE IN THERE!

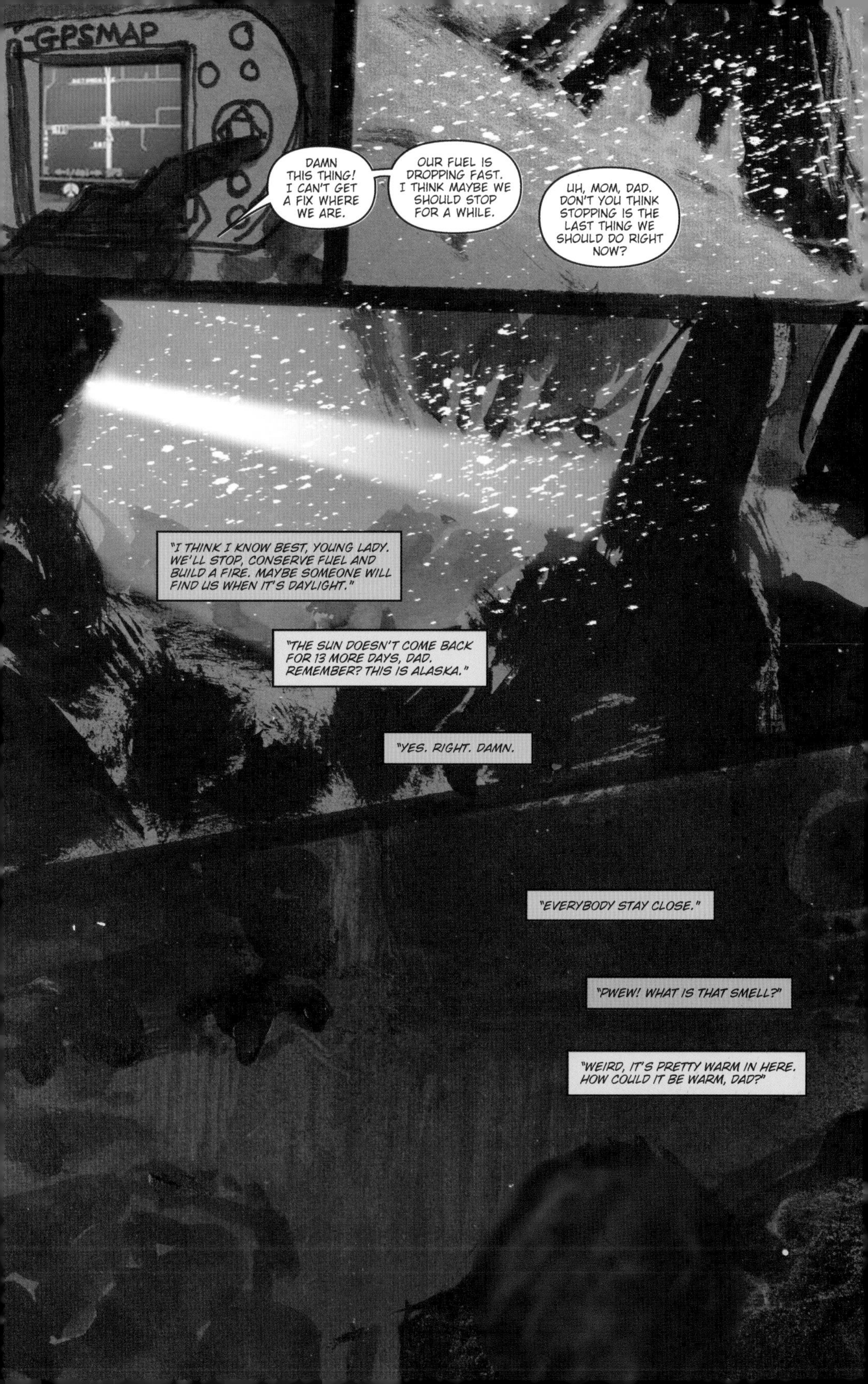
GPSMAP
DAMN THIS THING! I CAN'T GET A FIX WHERE WE ARE.
OUR FUEL IS DROPPING FAST. I THINK MAYBE WE SHOULD STOP FOR A WHILE.
UH, MOM, DAD. DON'T YOU THINK STOPPING IS THE LAST THING WE SHOULD DO RIGHT NOW?
"I THINK I KNOW BEST, YOUNG LADY. WE'LL STOP, CONSERVE FUEL AND BUILD A FIRE. MAYBE SOMEONE WILL FIND US WHEN IT'S DAYLIGHT."
"THE SUN DOESN'T COME BACK FOR 13 MORE DAYS, DAD. REMEMBER? THIS IS ALASKA."
"YES. RIGHT. DAMN.
"EVERYBODY STAY CLOSE."
"PWEW! WHAT IS THAT SMELL?"
"WEIRD, IT'S PRETTY WARM IN HERE. HOW COULD IT BE WARM, DAD?"

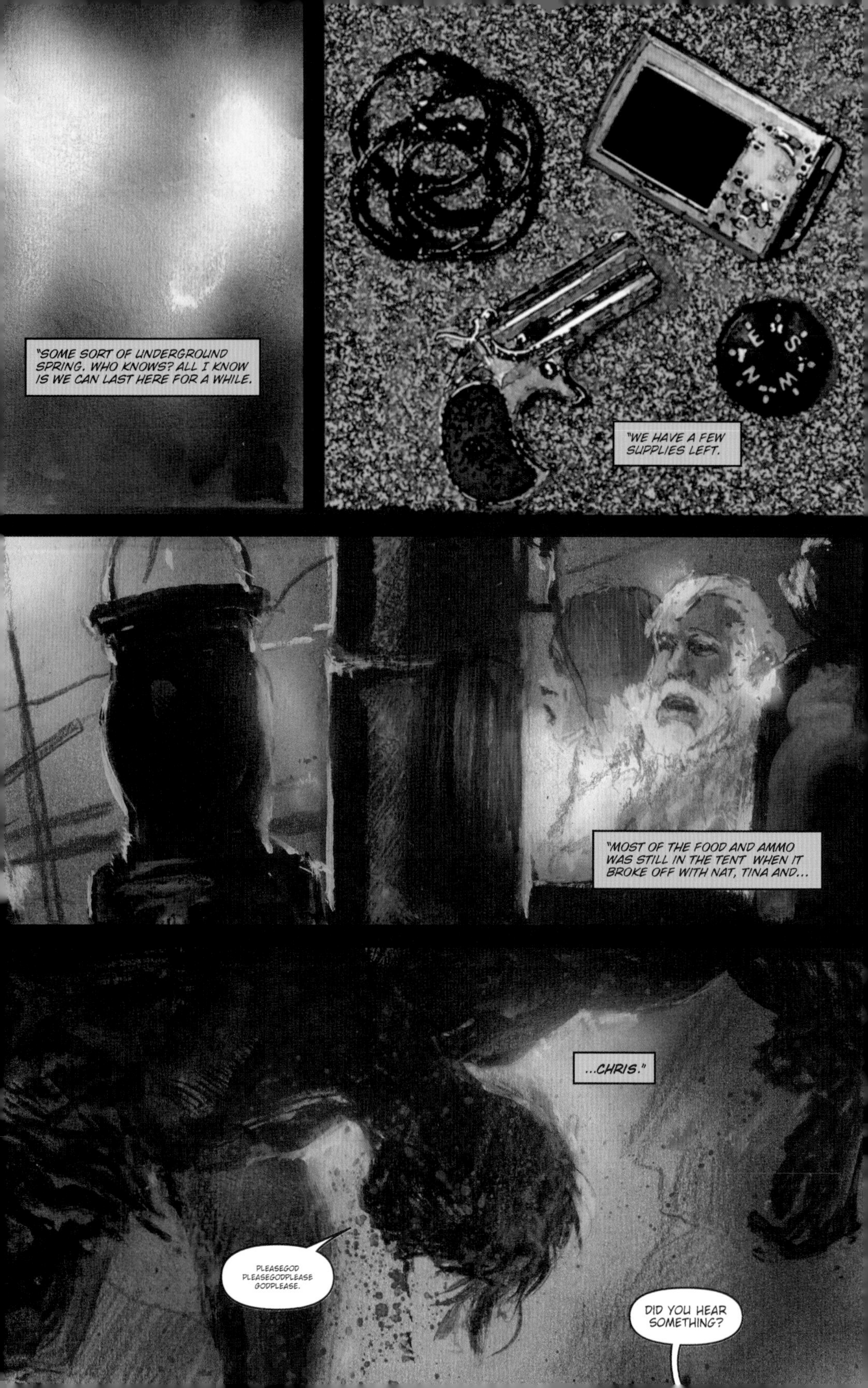
"SOME SORT OF UNDERGROUND SPRING. WHO KNOWS? ALL I KNOW IS WE CAN LAST HERE FOR A WHILE.
"WE HAVE A FEW SUPPLIES LEFT.
E S W N
"MOST OF THE FOOD AND AMMO WAS STILL IN THE TENT WHEN IT BROKE OFF WITH NAT, TINA AND...
...CHRIS."
PLEASEGOD PLEASEGODPLEASE GODPLEASE.
DID YOU HEAR SOMETHING?

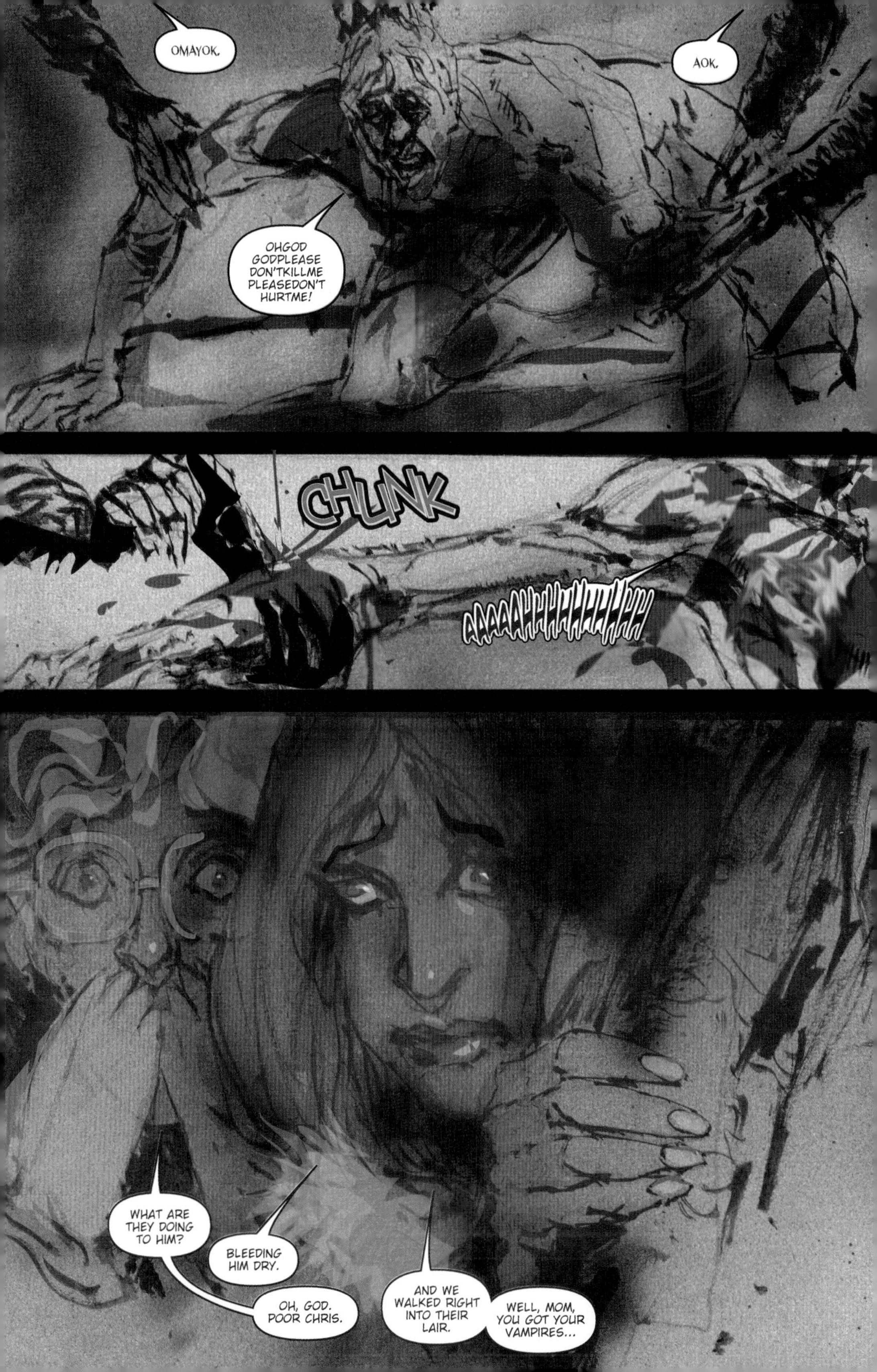
OMAYOK.
AOK.
OHGOD GODPLEASE DON'TKILLME PLEASEDON'T HURTME!
CHUNK
AAAAAHHHHHHHHHHH
WHAT ARE THEY DOING TO HIM?
BLEEDING HIM DRY.
OH, GOD. POOR CHRIS.
AND WE WALKED RIGHT INTO THEIR LAIR.
WELL, MOM, YOU GOT YOUR VAMPIRES...

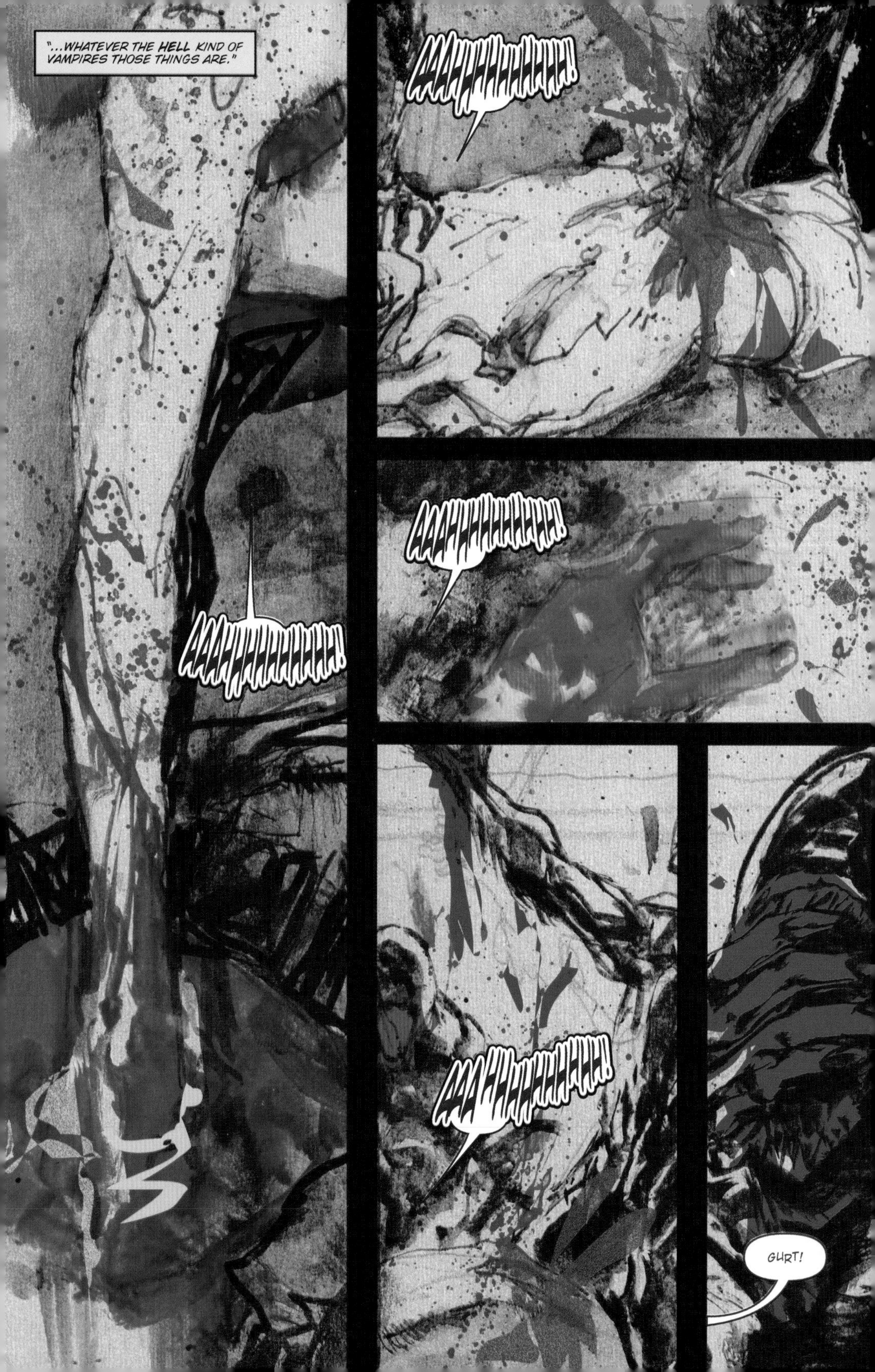
"...WHATEVER THE **HELL** KIND OF VAMPIRES THOSE THINGS ARE."
AAAHHHHHHHHHH!
AAAHHHHHHHHHH!
AAAHHHHHHHHHH!
AAAHHHHHHHHHH!
GURT!

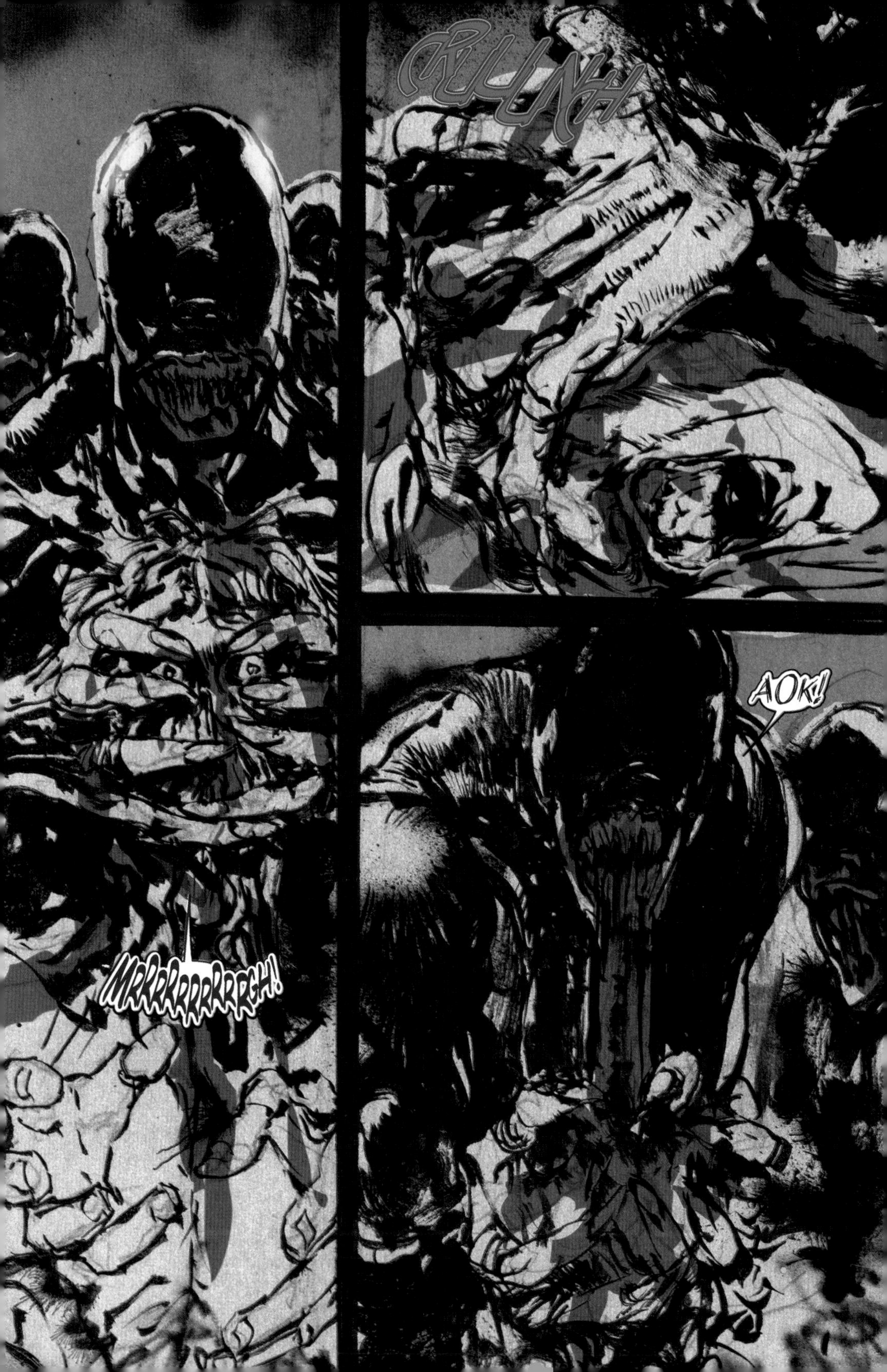
CRUNCH
MRRRRRRRRRRGH!
AOK!

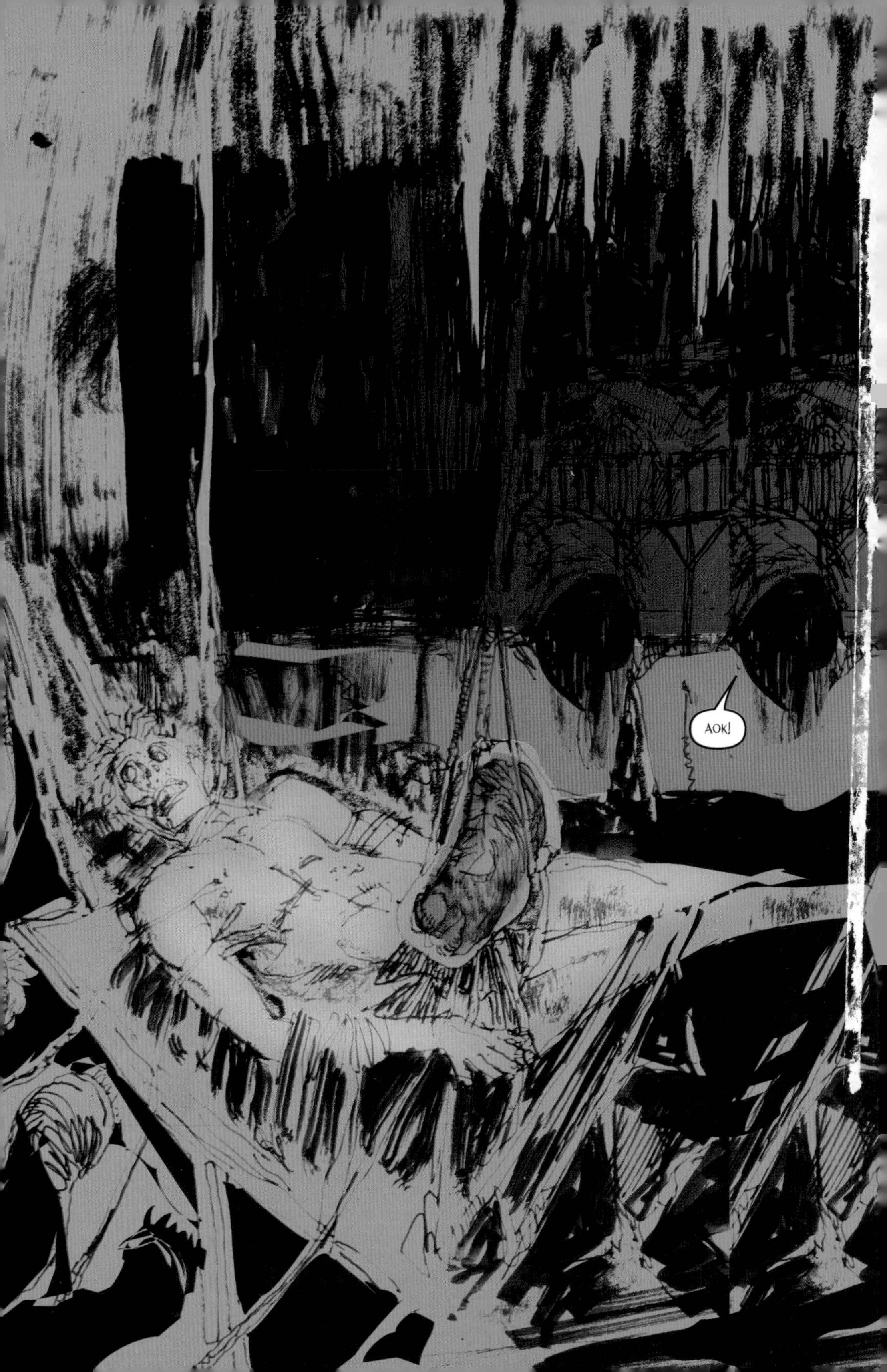

AOK!

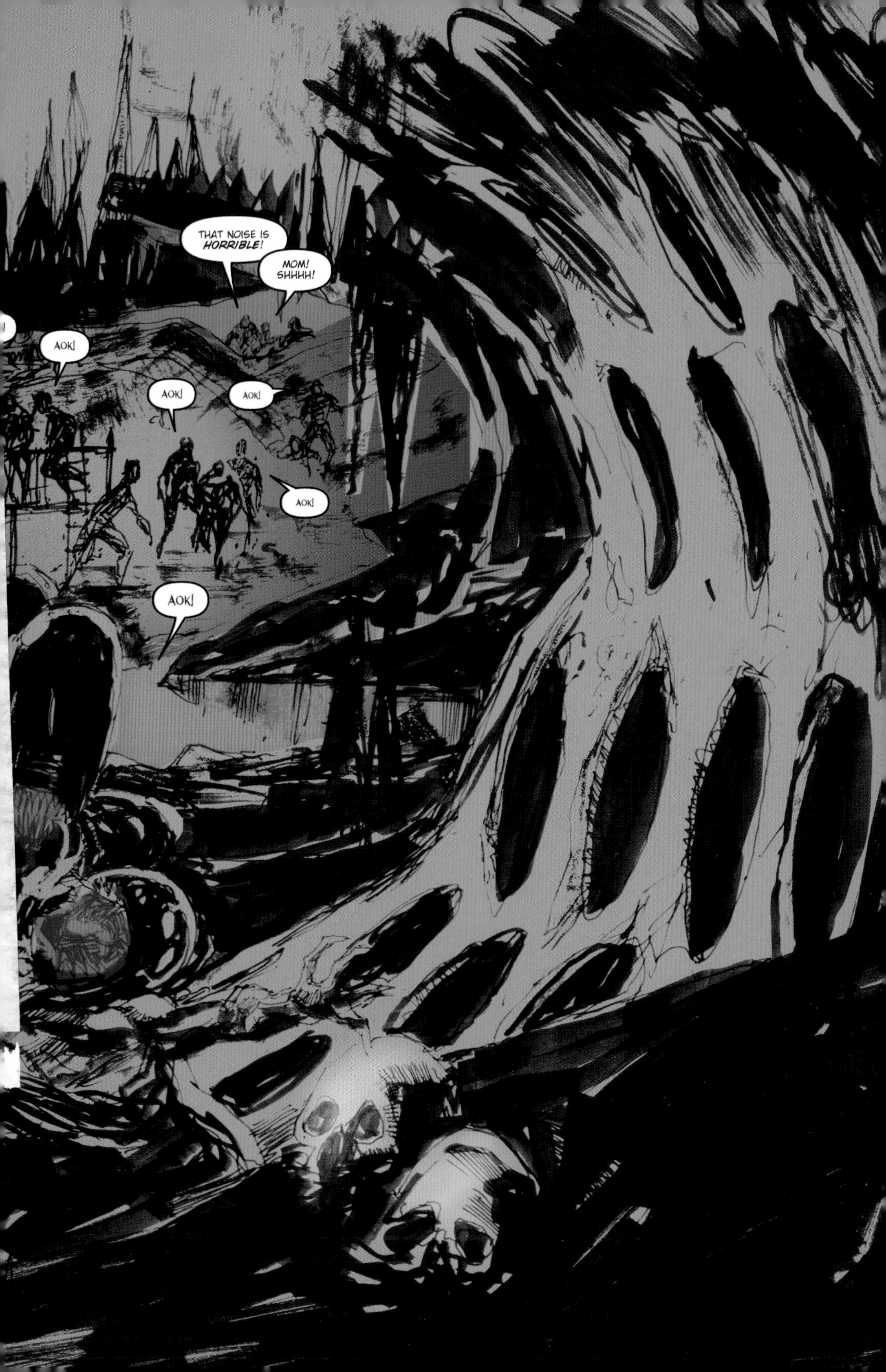
THAT NOISE IS *HORRIBLE*!
MOM! SHHHH!
AOK!
AOK!
AOK!
AOK!
AOK!

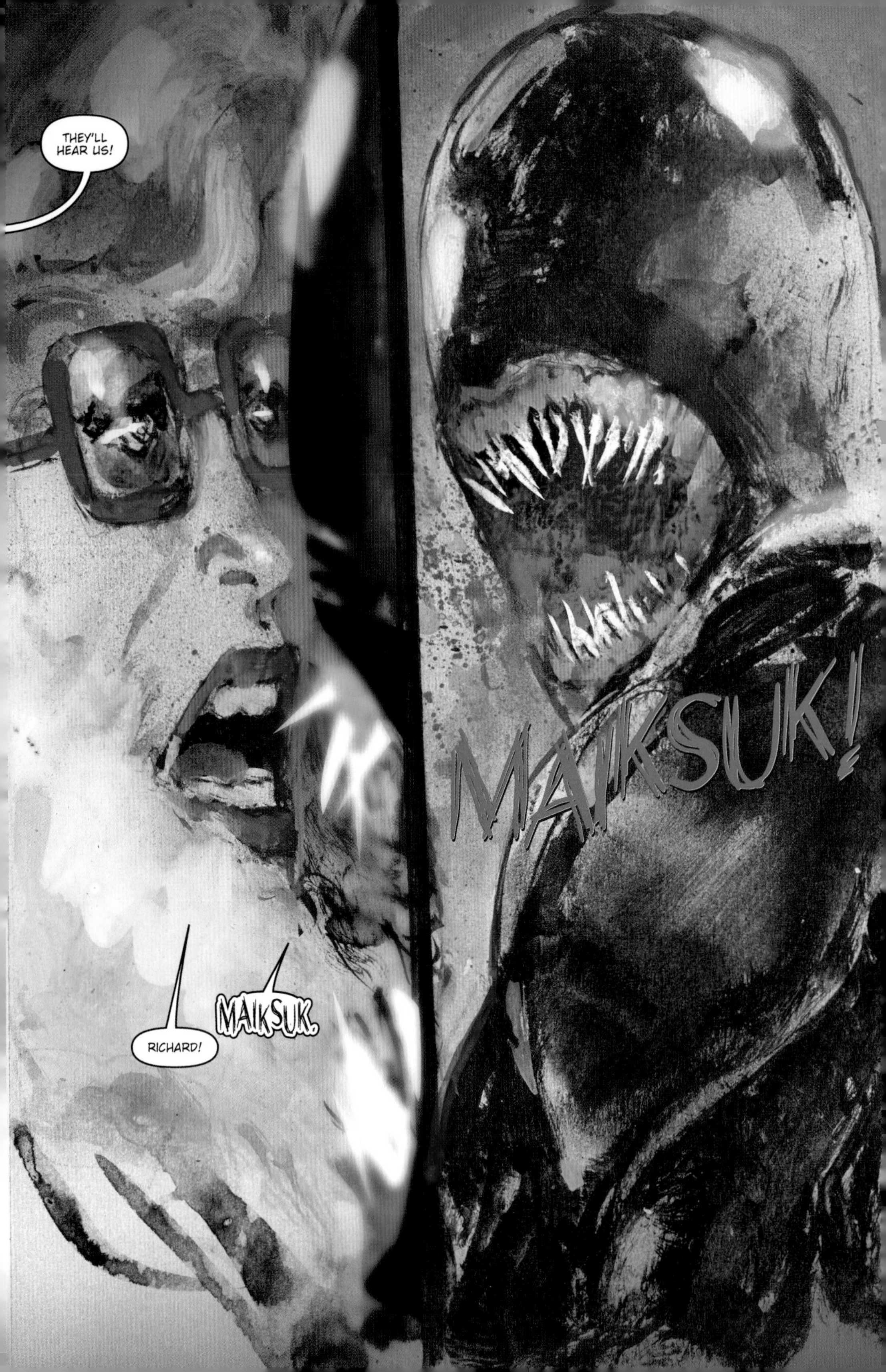
THEY'LL HEAR US!
RICHARD!
MAIKSUK.
MAIKSUK!

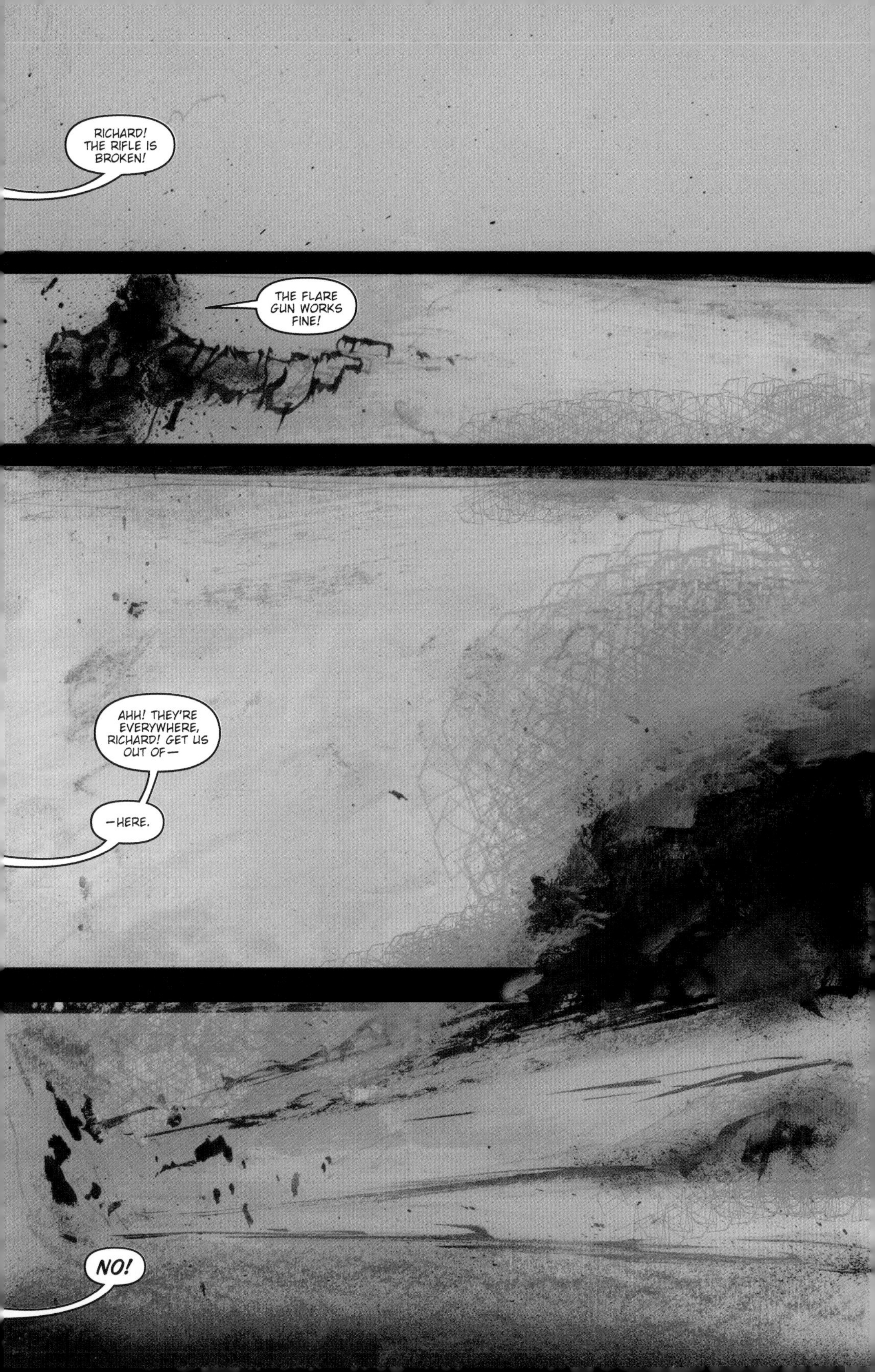
RICHARD! THE RIFLE IS BROKEN!
THE FLARE GUN WORKS FINE!
AHH! THEY'RE EVERYWHERE, RICHARD! GET US OUT OF—
—HERE.
NO!

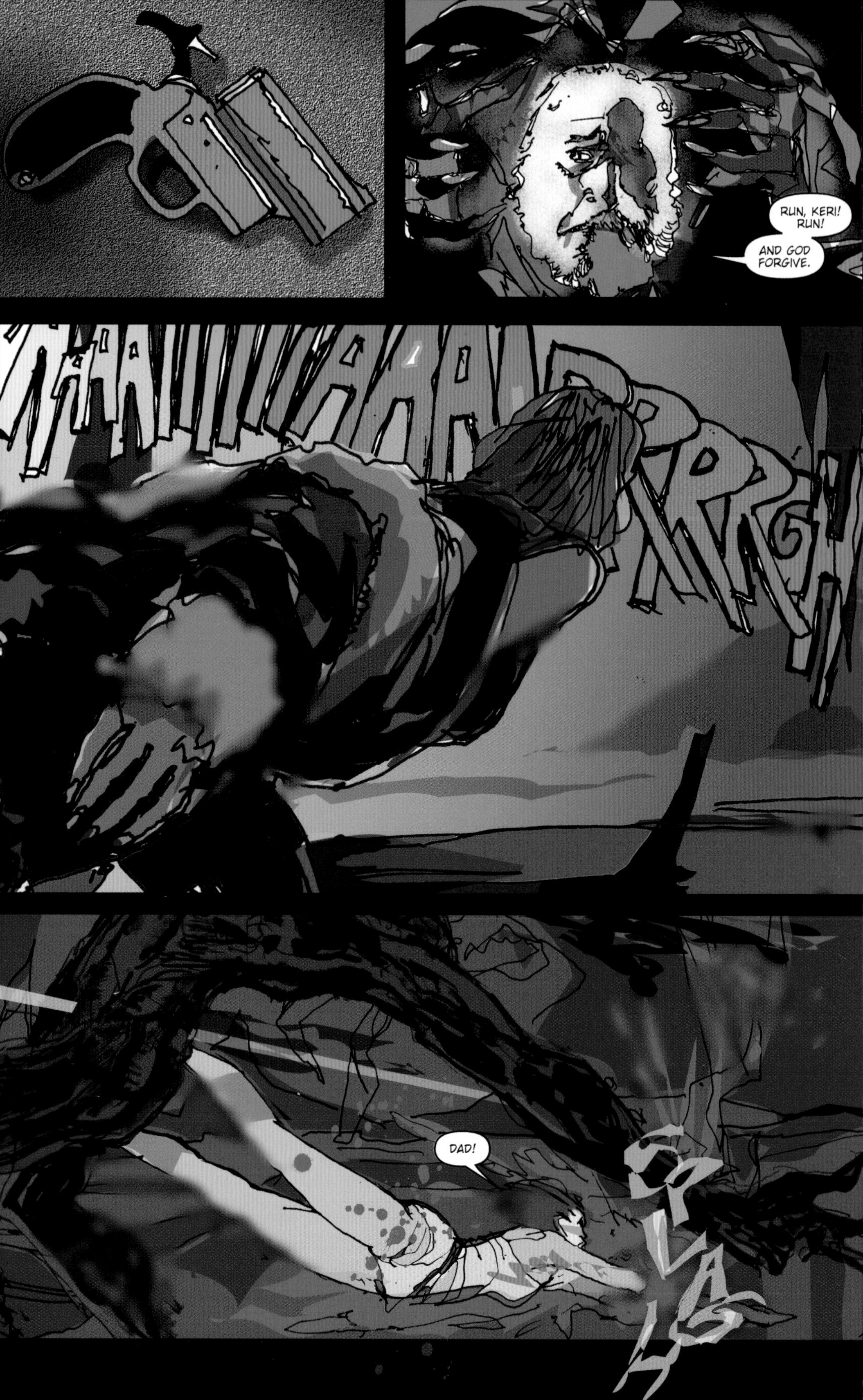
RUN, KERI! RUN!
AND GOD FORGIVE.
DAD!

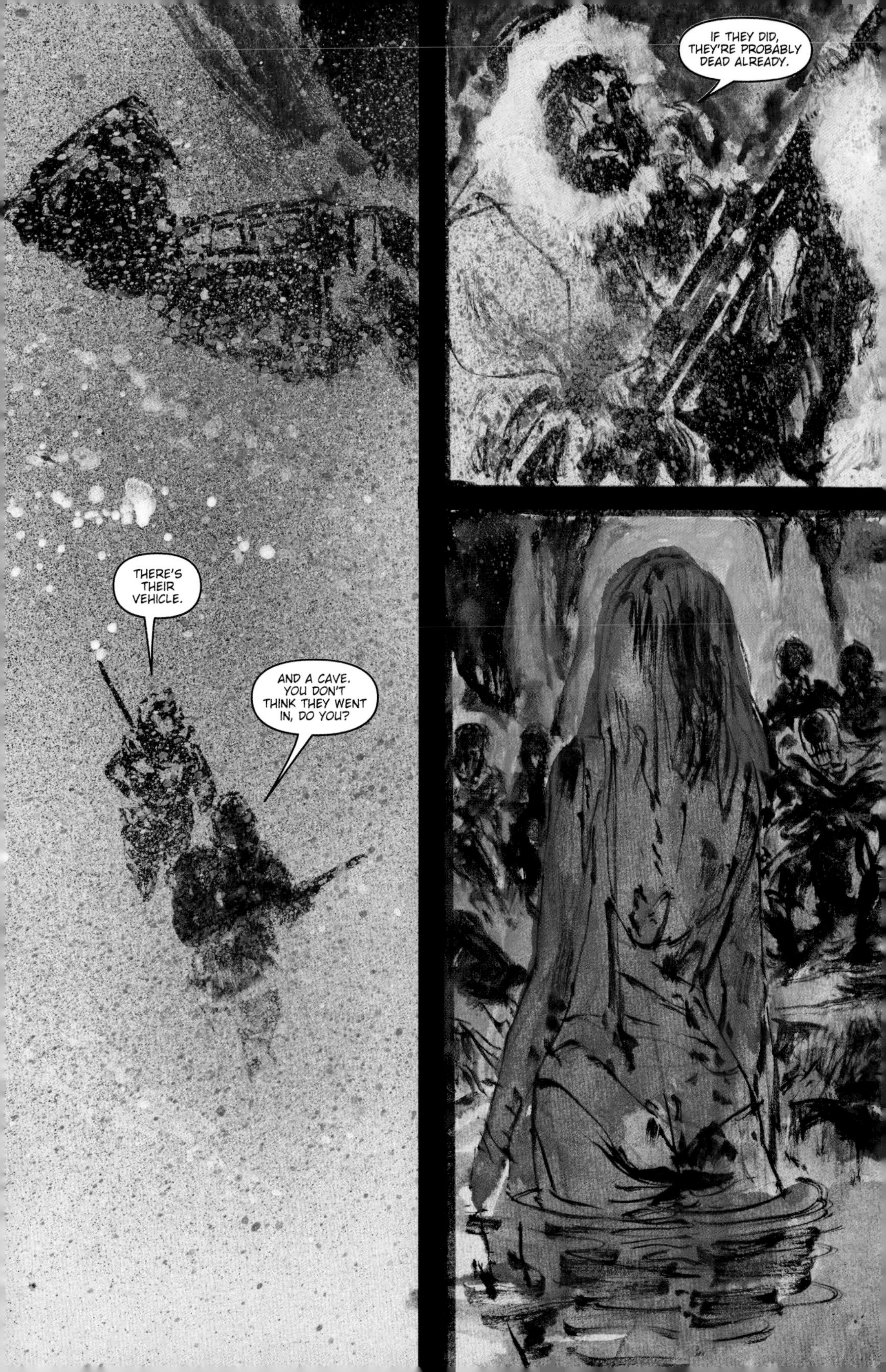
THERE'S THEIR VEHICLE.
AND A CAVE. YOU DON'T THINK THEY WENT IN, DO YOU?
IF THEY DID, THEY'RE PROBABLY DEAD ALREADY.

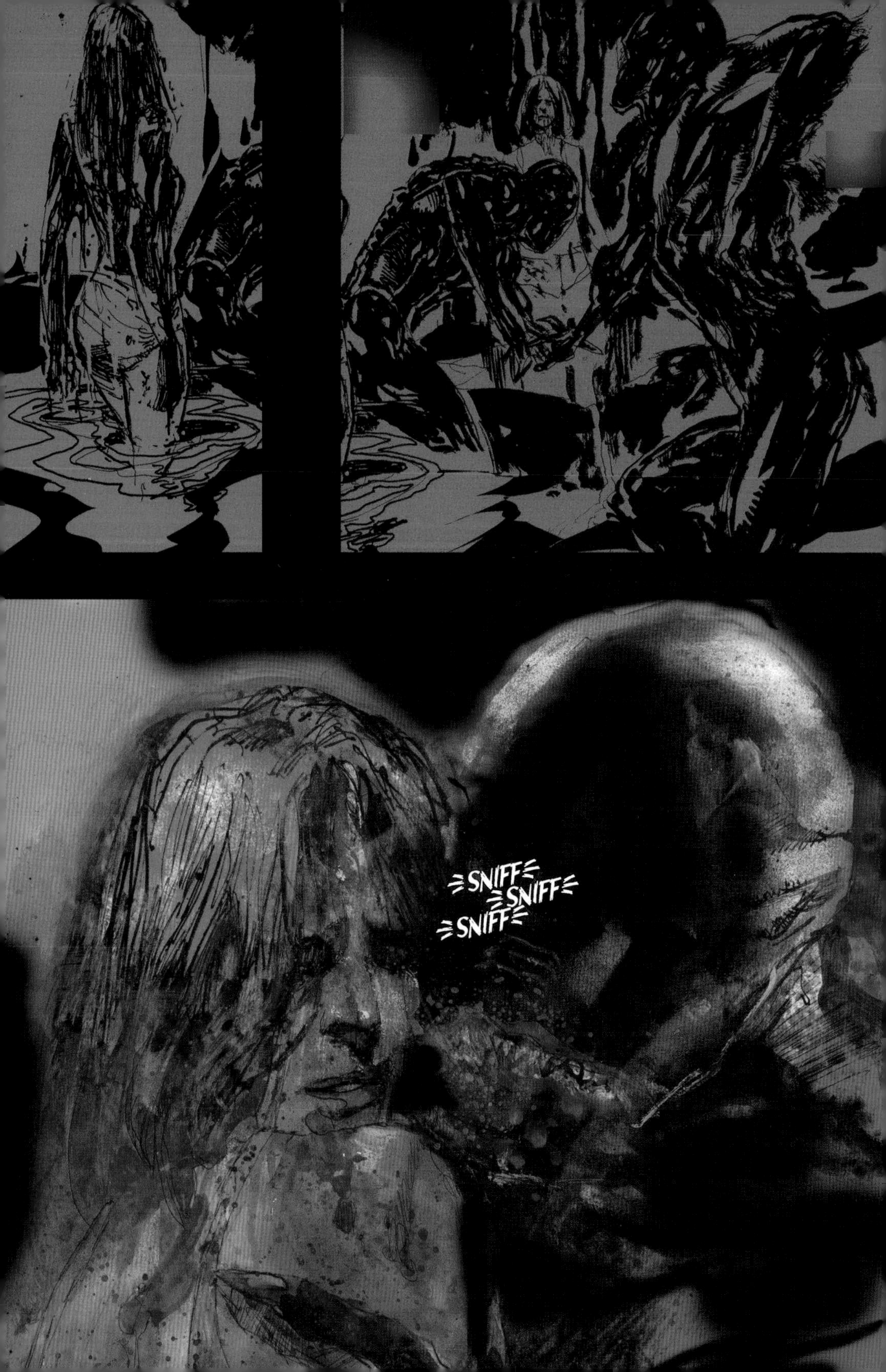
SNIFF
SNIFF
SNIFF

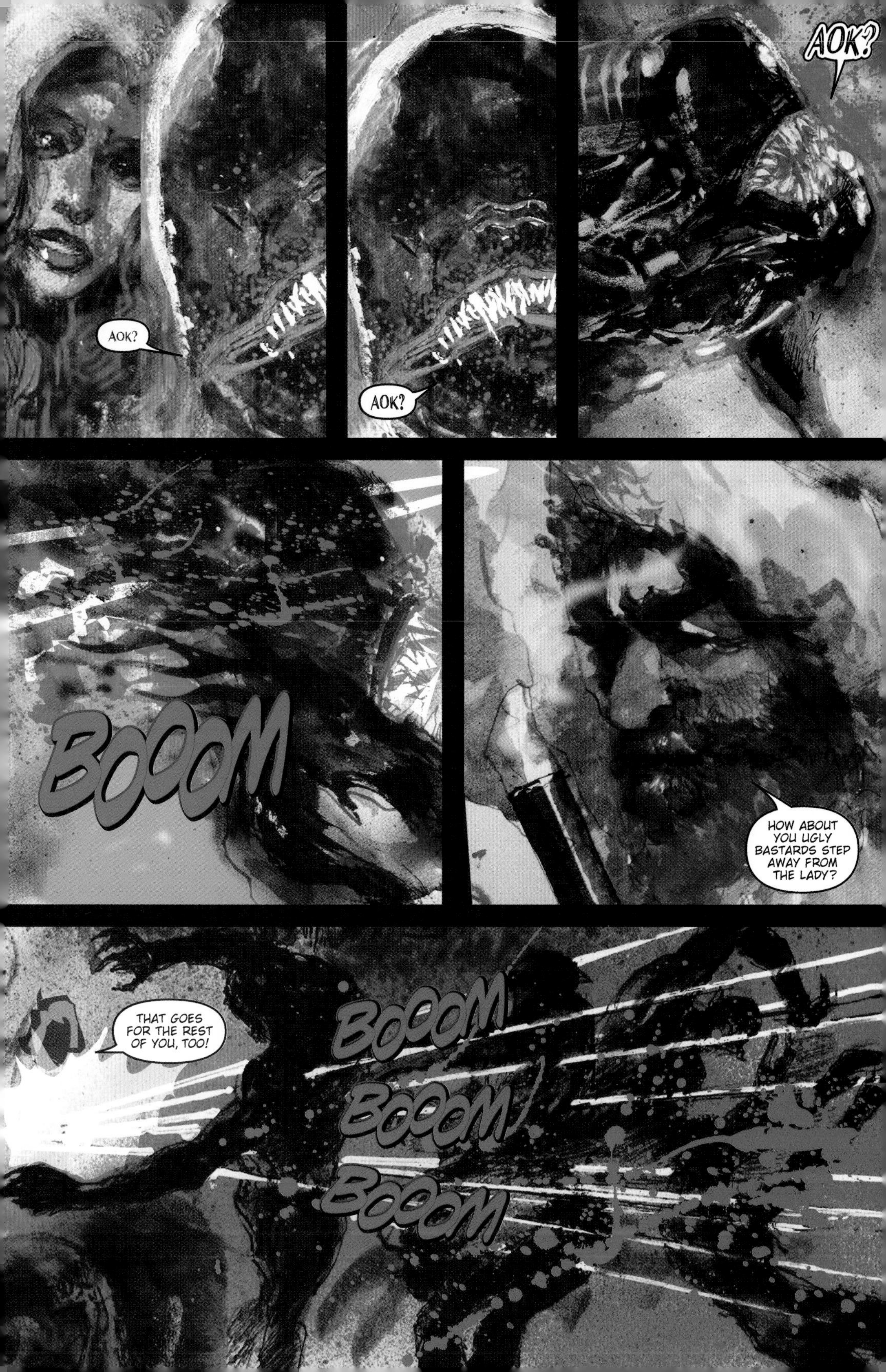
AOK?
AOK?
AOK?
BOOOM
HOW ABOUT YOU UGLY BASTARDS STEP AWAY FROM THE LADY?
THAT GOES FOR THE REST OF YOU, TOO!
BOOOM
BOOOM
BOOOM

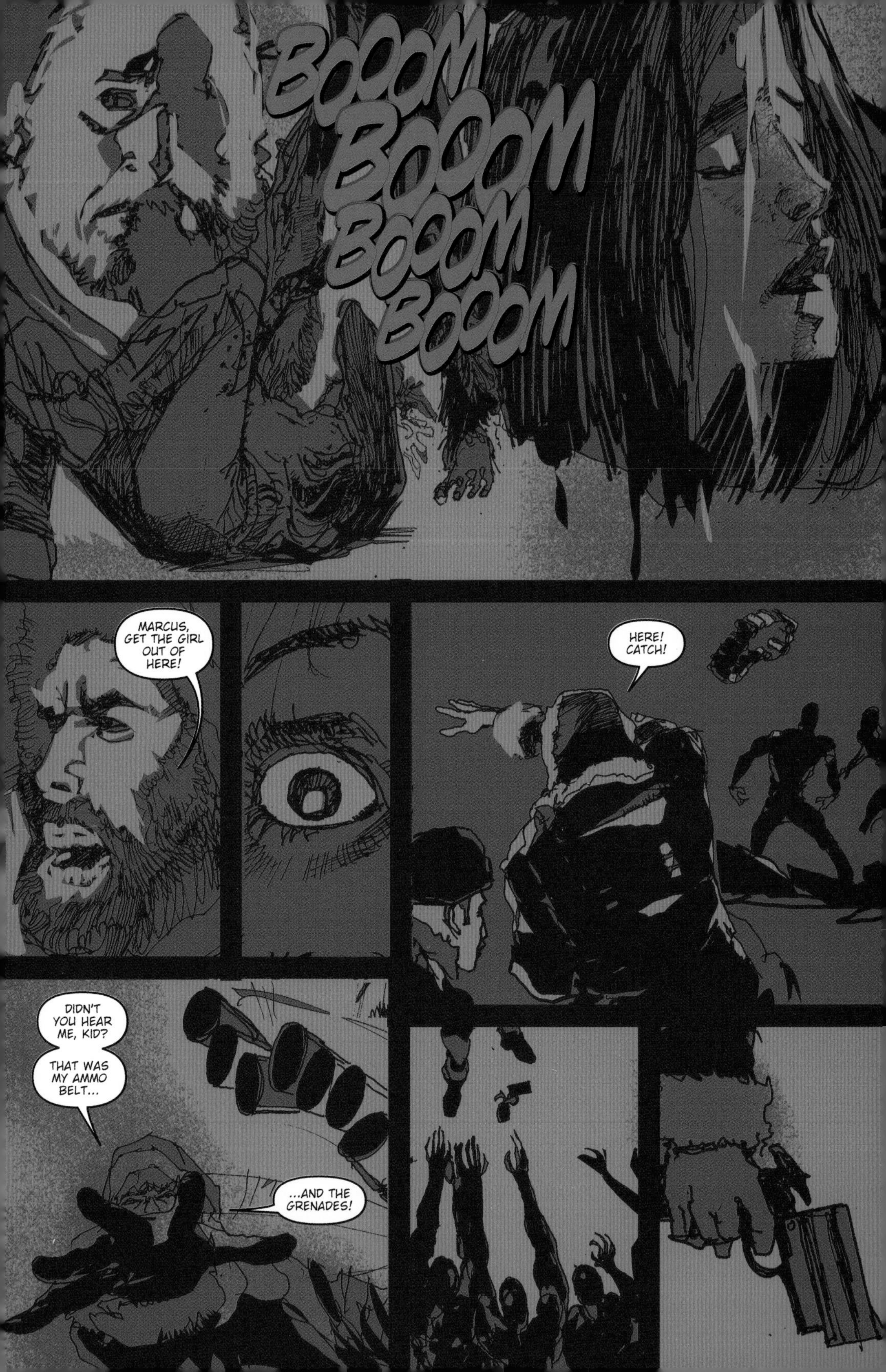

BOOOM BOOOM BOOOM BOOOM
MARCUS, GET THE GIRL OUT OF HERE!
HERE! CATCH!
DIDN'T YOU HEAR ME, KID?
THAT WAS MY AMMO BELT...
...AND THE GRENADES!

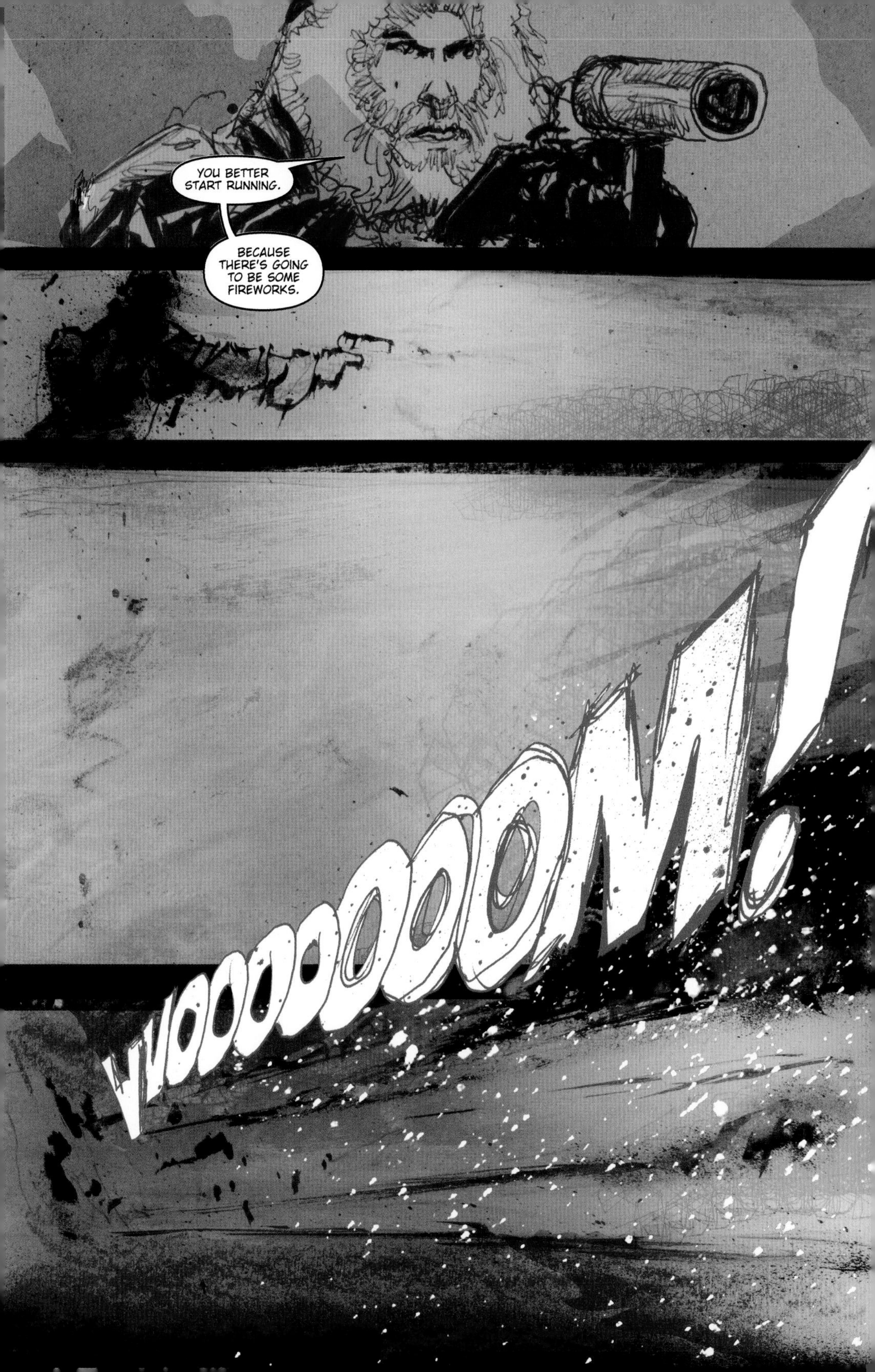
YOU BETTER START RUNNING.
BECAUSE THERE'S GOING TO BE SOME FIREWORKS.
VVOOOOOOOOM!!

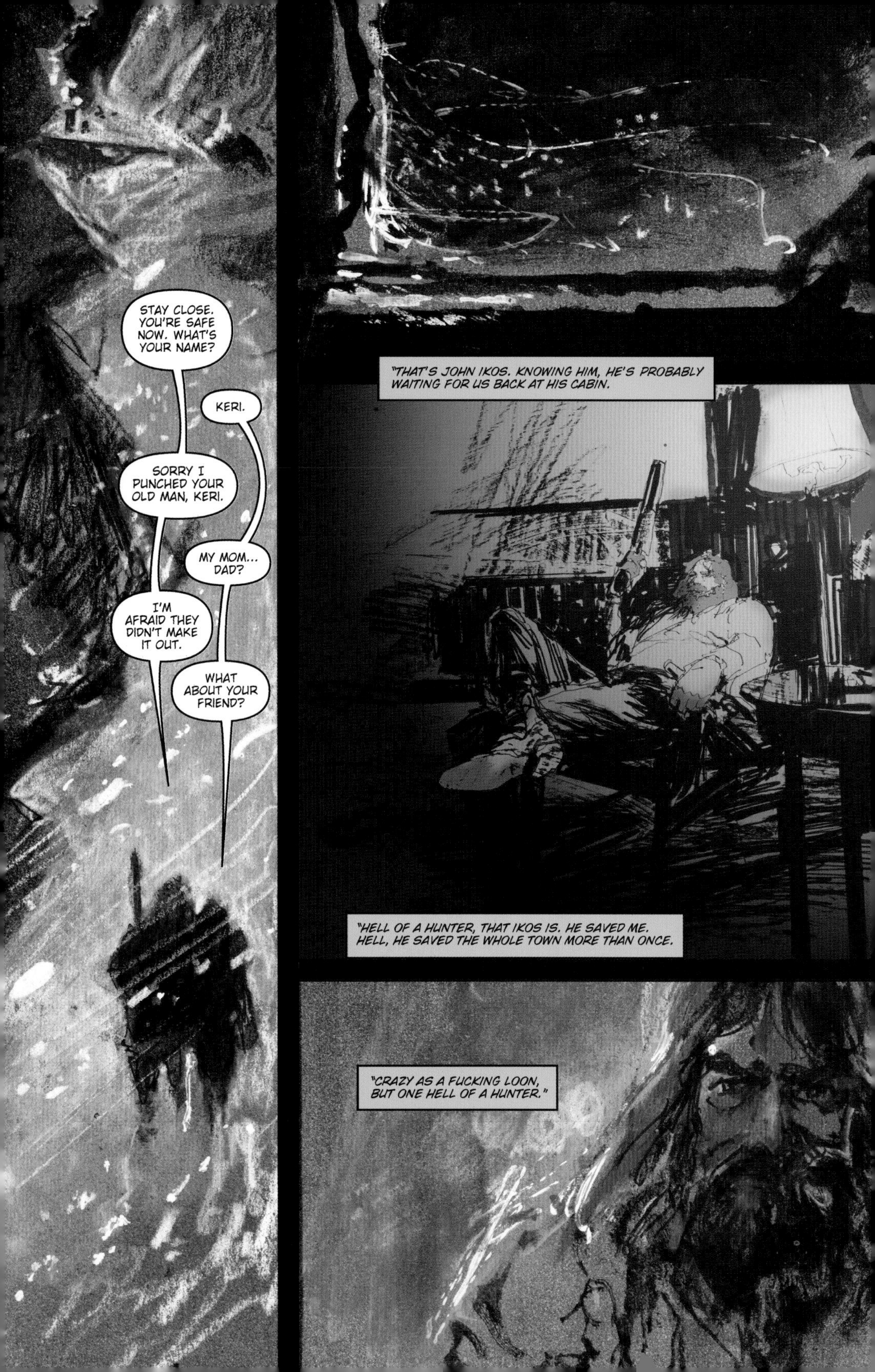
STAY CLOSE. YOU'RE SAFE NOW. WHAT'S YOUR NAME?
KERI.
SORRY I PUNCHED YOUR OLD MAN, KERI.
MY MOM... DAD?
I'M AFRAID THEY DIDN'T MAKE IT OUT.
WHAT ABOUT YOUR FRIEND?
"THAT'S JOHN IKOS. KNOWING HIM, HE'S PROBABLY WAITING FOR US BACK AT HIS CABIN.
"HELL OF A HUNTER, THAT IKOS IS. HE SAVED ME. HELL, HE SAVED THE WHOLE TOWN MORE THAN ONCE.
"CRAZY AS A FUCKING LOON, BUT ONE HELL OF A HUNTER."

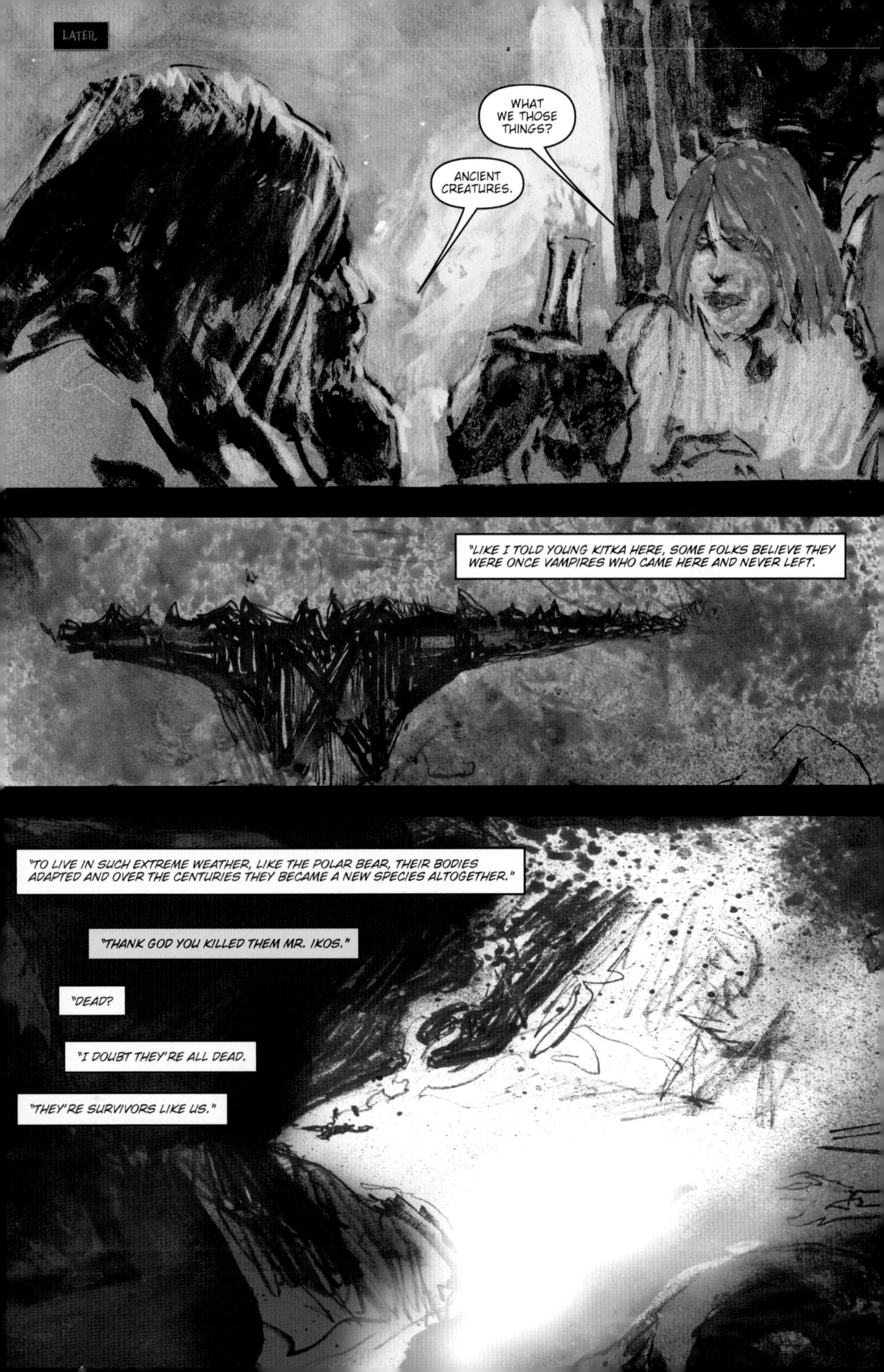
LATER.
WHAT WE THOSE THINGS?
ANCIENT CREATURES.
"LIKE I TOLD YOUNG KITKA HERE, SOME FOLKS BELIEVE THEY WERE ONCE VAMPIRES WHO CAME HERE AND NEVER LEFT.
"TO LIVE IN SUCH EXTREME WEATHER, LIKE THE POLAR BEAR, THEIR BODIES ADAPTED AND OVER THE CENTURIES THEY BECAME A NEW SPECIES ALTOGETHER."
"THANK GOD YOU KILLED THEM MR. IKOS."
"DEAD?
"I DOUBT THEY'RE ALL DEAD.
"THEY'RE SURVIVORS LIKE US."

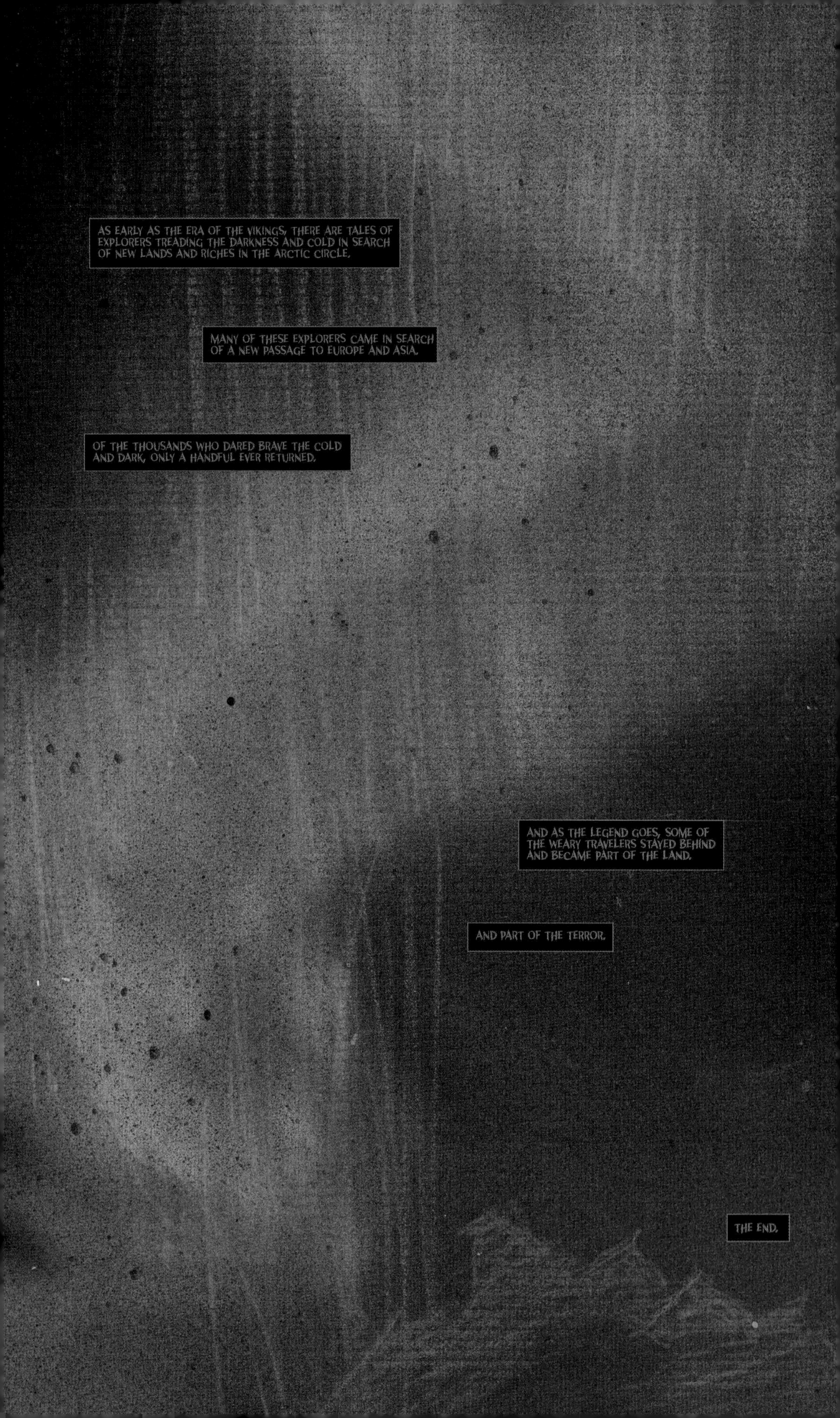

AS EARLY AS THE ERA OF THE VIKINGS, THERE ARE TALES OF EXPLORERS TREADING THE DARKNESS AND COLD IN SEARCH OF NEW LANDS AND RICHES IN THE ARCTIC CIRCLE.
MANY OF THESE EXPLORERS CAME IN SEARCH OF A NEW PASSAGE TO EUROPE AND ASIA.
OF THE THOUSANDS WHO DARED BRAVE THE COLD AND DARK, ONLY A HANDFUL EVER RETURNED.
AND AS THE LEGEND GOES, SOME OF THE WEARY TRAVELERS STAYED BEHIND AND BECAME PART OF THE LAND.
AND PART OF THE TERROR.
THE END.

STEVE · NILES
AND
SIENKIEWICZ

THIRTY DAYS of NIGHT

HE REAL THING   BURROW BARROW

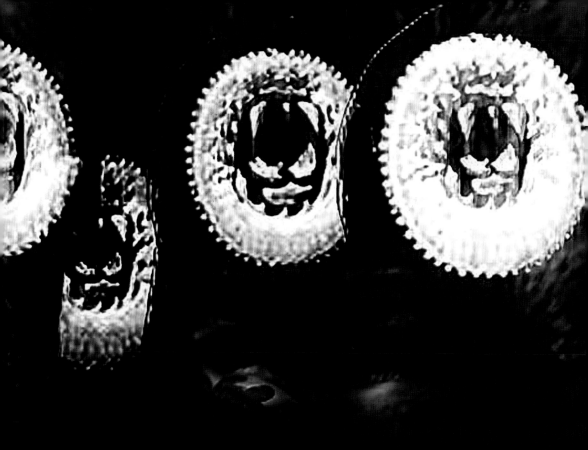

30 Days of Night:
Beyond Barrow
#1 Script
steve niles

0 DAYS OF NIGHT:

EYOND BARROW

1

teve Niles

007

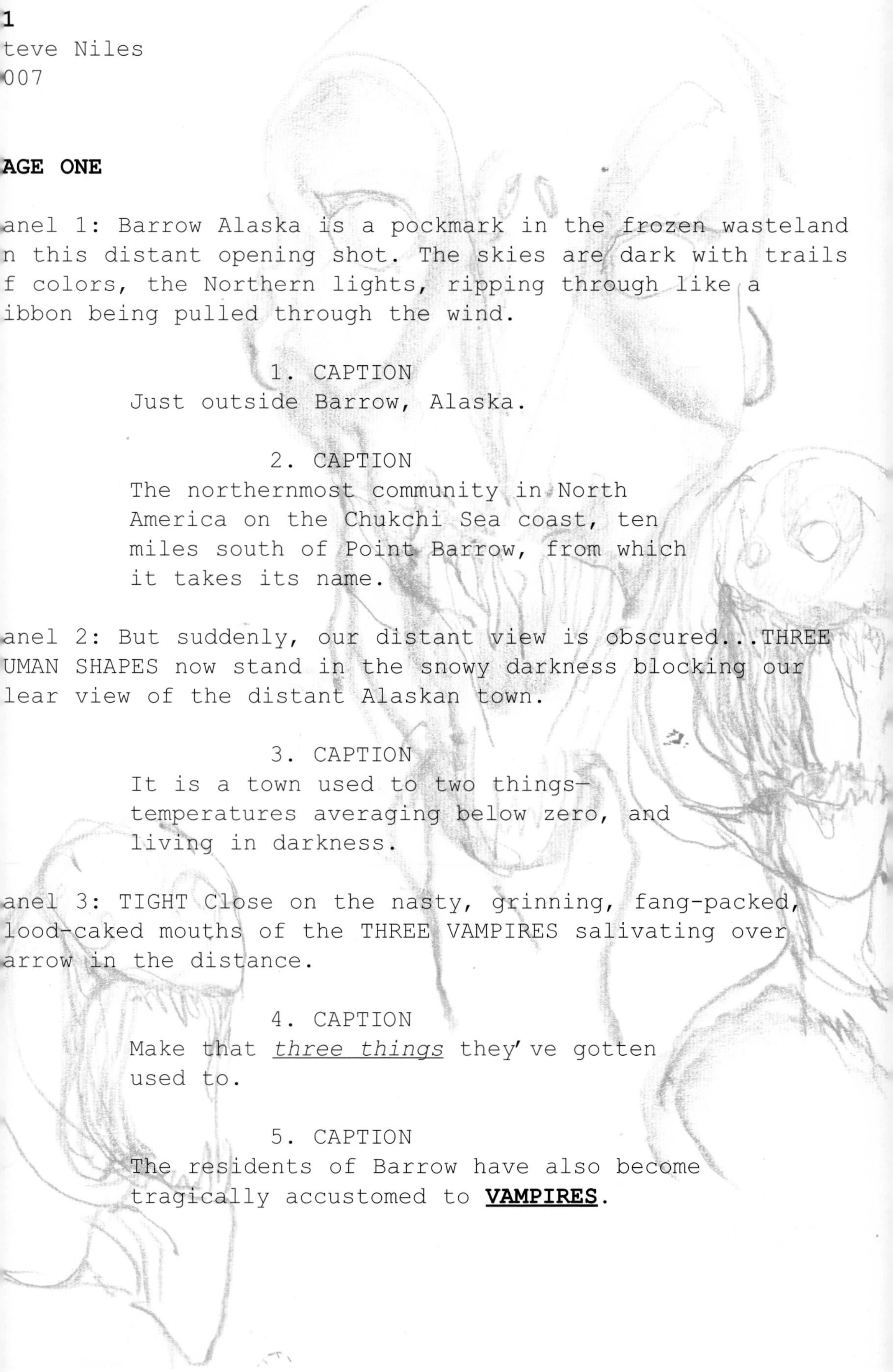

AGE ONE

anel 1: Barrow Alaska is a pockmark in the frozen wasteland n this distant opening shot. The skies are dark with trails f colors, the Northern lights, ripping through like a ibbon being pulled through the wind.

1. CAPTION
Just outside Barrow, Alaska.

2. CAPTION
The northernmost community in North America on the Chukchi Sea coast, ten miles south of Point Barrow, from which it takes its name.

anel 2: But suddenly, our distant view is obscured...THREE UMAN SHAPES now stand in the snowy darkness blocking our lear view of the distant Alaskan town.

3. CAPTION
It is a town used to two things—temperatures averaging below zero, and living in darkness.

anel 3: TIGHT Close on the nasty, grinning, fang-packed, lood-caked mouths of the THREE VAMPIRES salivating over arrow in the distance.

4. CAPTION
Make that _three things_ they’ve gotten used to.

5. CAPTION
The residents of Barrow have also become tragically accustomed to **VAMPIRES**.

PAGES TWO & THREE

SPREAD: High above the entire vast scene is revealed to us
and it's as much an atmospheric landscape shot as it is a
storytelling spread; we can see THREE main things in this
spread. Where and how they fall is up to you. At one end of
the spread is the town of Barrow. We can see the lights of
the town surrounded by fence and gate and a small LANDING
STRIP and AIRPORT. On the other end we see the MOUNTAINS and
just at the bottom we can see the figures of the three
VAMPIRES (all very Euro trash) trudging *away* from the hills
they've just crossed. Maybe we can see their wake in the
snow, their footprints (more like drag marks!) coming down
the side of the mountains slope. There are no trees in
sight, just mountains, snow, ice and rolling tundra.
HOWEVER, at the bottom of the slope just short of where the
vampires are trudging we can see ODD grey and black rocks
scattered about.

> 1. CAPTION
> The sun does not set between May 10th
> and August 2nd, and does not rise
> between November 18th and January 24th
> each winter.

> 2. CAPTION
> The last day the sun rose was 15 days
> ago.

> 3. CAPTION
> It will remain dark for at least another
> 15 days.

> 4. CAPTION
> For creatures who fear the light and
> thirst for blood, Barrow and the entire
> Artic Circle are heaven on earth.

> 5. CAPTION
> **Hell** on earth, if you are human.

PAGE FOUR

Panel 1: Close in on the three vampires trudging through the
vast open tundra with the huge sky above and the mountains
behind. These are not the romantic vampires of novels. These
vampires, though wearing pretty trendy cloths, are like
living rats. Their clothes are stained with blood and

ipped, their hair matted and their flesh pocked and whitish
yellow like a corpse. Their eyes are lifeless, pinned and
cruel. The leader has long stringy black hair and blood
dried and caked on his lips. The second is a WOMAN wearing a
tattered black gothic dress. The third is a BLONDE MAN
wearing a jean jacket and Dickies. He is covered with dried
blood from victims past. Here they are standing squinting in
the harsh wind at the distant Barrow.

                    1. WOMAN
          We should not be here.

                    2. LEADER
          We will not stay long. Just long enough
          to feed.

Panel 2: Blonde licks his lips SLICING his own tongue on his
razor rows of teeth.

                    3. BLONDE
          And fill our bellies.

Panel 3: Focus in on Leader and Woman vampires as they argue
while Blonde vamp stands in the background looking ahead at
the distant lights of Barrow.

                    4. WOMAN
          The townspeople are prepared now and the
          elders are watching. Attacking this
          place is forbidden.

                    5. LEADER
          So you've been saying... and yet you
          followed me here. So spare me your last
          minute panic.

                    6. LEADER 2
          We will invade, feed and then leave.
          Nobody, not even our own will be the
          wiser.

Panel 4: Cutting away from the arguing vampires, we focus on
the Blonde who is facing Barrow, in the distance, and
squinting into the icy wind which pounds against his sickly
flesh.

                    7. BLONDE
          Hey...

Panel 5: The other vampires turn from their conversation and all three look at the LIGHTS FROM A PLANE heading down towards the Barrow Airport, far in the distance.

> 8. BLONDE
> A plane is landing.

> 9. LEADER
> Let them come.

PAGE FIVE

Panel 1: Pulling back we can see the three vampires watching the lights head down towards Barrow in the distance. Around them is nothing but flat icy ground covered with snow and these ODD black and gray STONES scattered about.

> 1. LEADER
> More blood for us.

Panel 2: Leaving the Woman and Blonde vampires standing, the greasy-haired Leader trudges on towards Barrow and the lights that still hang in the air above the far away landing strip.

> 2. LEADER
> Now, let's keep moving. I am starving.

Panel 3: The woman is speaking to the departing Leader and starting to walk herself, but she is also glancing down at one of the odd stones. If she was looking closely she would see that the snow on the stone was thin and MELTING, water running over the sides like tears.

> 3. WOMAN
> On that we are agreed.

Panel 4: One of the "stones" is in the foreground, the snow melting and running over its edges. In the background we see the Woman and the Leader walking off towards the lights of Barrow as the Blonde glances nervously back over his shoulder.

> 4. SOUNDFX (small)
> _Ssssssssss_

> 5. BLONDE
> What the…?!

AGES SIX & SEVEN, EIGHT & NINE

AGE DESCRIPTION: Okay, this one I hand to you completely. I
igure two pages should be enough to show the total
nnihilation of these three vampires.

here are several key points we want to see, or rather NOT
EE, in this scene. The main thing is that these creatures,
hese vampires who are cocky and have never been beaten, are
ttacked with such ferocity that they become afraid. Not
nly that, but they are being slashed and cut and beaten so
ast they cannot see their attackers.

his is a fast scary sequence with fear coming over the
ampires eyes...

..and remaining there when the last vampire is dragged
way, his hands outstretched and face mostly obscured by the
onsuming darkness as if he were being drowned in ink.

EW NOTE- an important element I forgot…lets show the
ampires, these three bloodsuckers who are coming to invade,
o from cocky -ain't-scared-of-nothin' to piss their pants
cared as they are stalked and killed by the feral vampires
e never see. It can be very cinematic, almost illustrated
irst person POV, where the fear of what's out there is made
ll the stronger by only seeing them via the fear in the
yes of creatures who are *never* afraid, and through the
esults of the violence. I can see a large image of the
ftermath, a cropped version of the earlier reveal with the
revious almost undisturbed white snow now a large black and
ed stain, kicked and dragged up dirt and ice and all of it
ragging away from us into the darkness. And where the rocks
reviously sat, the area is disturbed as though something
nfolded from it and leapt. But the oddest thing is the
ontrast; this horrible patch of gore, a severed hand, a jaw
ragment, an eye, surrounded by clean white and in the far
istance, Barrow glows, always lit when locked-down. And
here's the STEAM rising from the massacre patch, wisps
eminding the readers, this just happened.

creams and dialogue of terror will be added later.

                    1.   Leader
              There is something here…

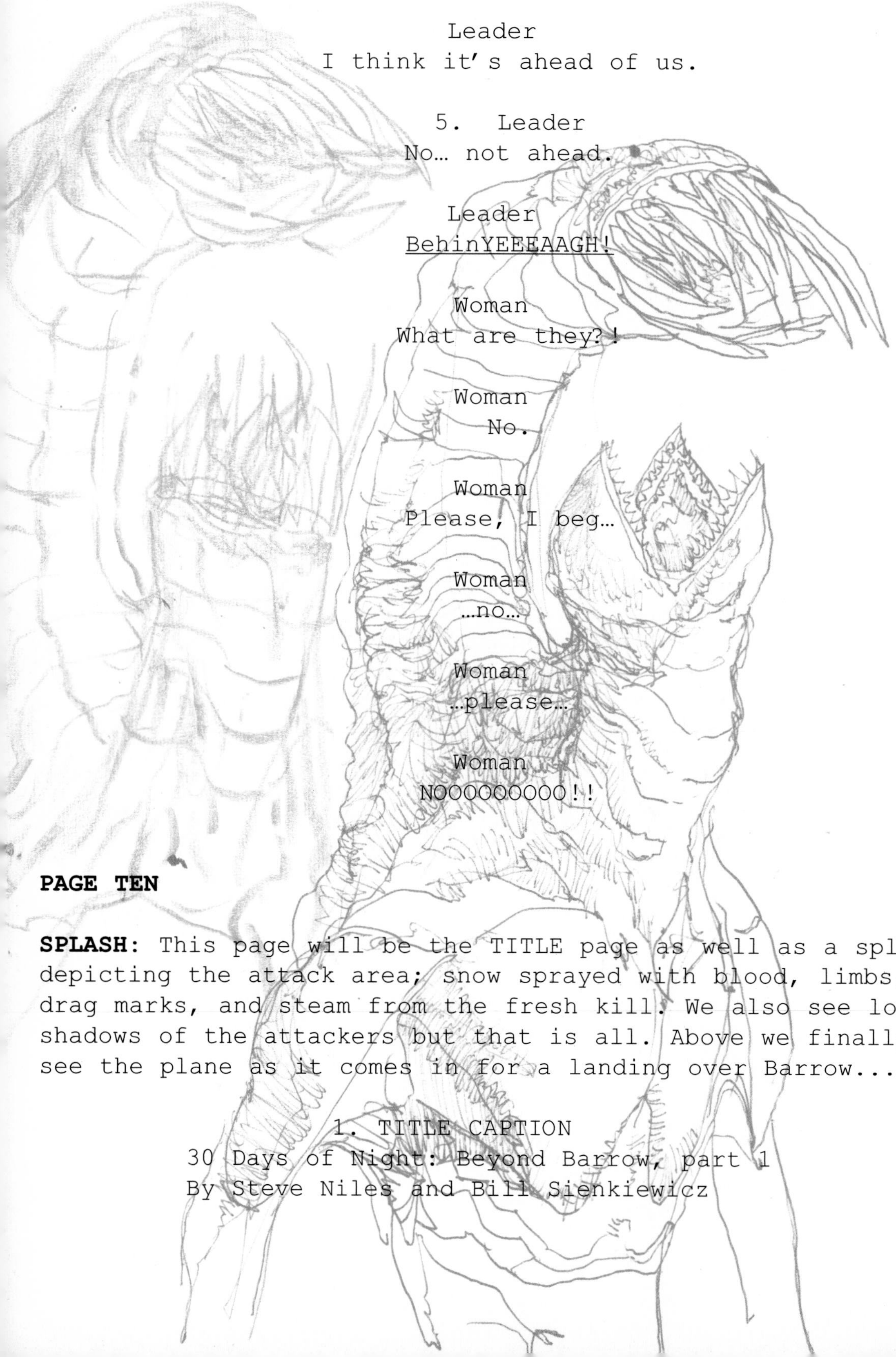

Leader
…do you sense it, too?

Woman
Y-yes…

Leader
I think it's ahead of us.

5. Leader
No… not ahead.

Leader
<u>BehinYEEEAAGH!</u>

Woman
What are they?!

Woman
No.

Woman
Please, I beg…

Woman
…no…

Woman
…please…

Woman
NOOOOOOOOO!!

PAGE TEN

SPLASH: This page will be the TITLE page as well as a splash depicting the attack area; snow sprayed with blood, limbs, drag marks, and steam from the fresh kill. We also see long shadows of the attackers but that is all. Above we finally see the plane as it comes in for a landing over Barrow...

1. TITLE CAPTION
30 Days of Night: Beyond Barrow, part 1
By Steve Niles and Bill Sienkiewicz

Panel 1: Open LARGE as we switch all the way to the BARROW AIRPORT/LANDING STRIP. The airport is little more than a warehouse next to a landing strip. The plane coming in is a large PRIVATE PLANE. Small enough to hold only six people, but large enough to haul a truck in cargo. Here the plane is touching down as airport operator, ROB HUEY (50's) stands by the main building watching nervously.

    1. CAPTION
Rob Huey had been running the Barrow
Airport for the better part of 10 years.

    2. CAPTION
He'd made it through the worst winters,
an IRS audit, and two divorces.

    3. CAPTION
He'd even survived both attacks.

Panel 2: The plane has landed as Rob flips OFF the landing lights.

    4. CAPTION
Now it seemed finances could be the
death of him.

    5. CAPTION
And that was why Rob Huey broke the law
and opened the airport during the dark
season.

    6. CAPTION
He felt like a world-class shit, but the
cash was just too good to pass up.

Panel 3: Our main characters begin to emerge from the plane...They are RICHARD DENNING, a billionaire and self proclaimed adventurer, who is the first to emerge. He's a Richard Branson type; Rich and full of himself.

    7. CAPTION
RICHARD DENNING, a billionaire and self-
proclaimed adventurer. He's in Barrow
for the thrill because he read vampires
were there.

                    8. RICHARD
     Well, here we are! The top of the world!

Panel 4: And the rest come down the stairs of the plane
following Richard and fighting the biting cold. First is
KELLY DENNING.

                    9. CAPTION
          KELLY DENNING, Richard's wife. Kelly
          showed him Stella's book and that's what
          got the idea rolling in his head. A
          couple years before, Richard and Kelly
          camped near Area 51 trying to get UFO
          pictures, and flew over the Bermuda
          Triangle last year. Nothing happened.

                    10. KELLY
          It's two in the afternoon and dark as
          midnight! How fun!

PAGE TWELVE

Panel 1: And now standing at the bottom of the stairs on the
tarmac are the rest of the crew: KERI DENNING, Richard and
Kelly's teen daughter. CHRIS MILLER and his girlfriend TINA.
NATE GILMORE and SCOTT POWELL. I'd love it if we could do a
large wide shot showing the whole crew and I'll put small
captions above them. How's that sound? Feel free to give
them each a panel. I'll keep this page short so you have
room to move.

                    1. CAPTION
          KERI DENNING, daughter of Richard and
          Kelly. Would rather be anywhere else in
          the world.

                    2. CAPTION
          CHRIS MILLER and his latest girlfriend,
          TINA MARROW. They came along because
          they see themselves as open for
          anything. Unfortunately, their
          adventures haven't gotten much further
          than drunken Vegas weekends and a spa in
          Arizona where Tina cheated on Chris and
          had sex with a masseuse.

                    3. CAPTION
          NAT GILMORE. He works for Richard. He

had no choice but to come along on this
ridiculous fool's errand.

        4. CAPTION
SCOTT POWELL. He's Richard's best friend
from college and introduced Chris and
Richard. He's slept with both Tina and
Kelly. Scott likes guns and photography
and plans to be the first human to
photograph a real and for true
vampire... dead or alive.

Panel 2: Off to the side near the rear of the plane, the
cargo door is coming down like a ramp as Richard hands Rob
Huey a fat envelope of cash.

        5. RICHARD
    This should cover the landing, take off _and_ your
silence.

        6. ROB
    Deal. Are you going to need any transportation
while you're here in Barrow?

        7. RICHARD
    We don't plan on spending much time in town... and
I brought my own transportation.

Panel 3: REVEAL the super HUMMER with TANK TREADS where the
tires should be. Rob is wide-eyed, shocked and impressed.
Richard is smug as he eats up the glory.

        8. ROB
    Holy shit!

        9. RICHARD
    I bought it directly from the same
manufacturer who makes them for the
Alaskan National Guard. Of course, I had
all the bells and whistles added—
stereo, heat, video decks, and a full
bar.

        10. ROB
    Folks around here are lucky if we can
get chains on our tires or a rundown
snow-cat.

> ### 11. RICHARD
> Well, folks around here should invest their money better.

PAGE THIRTEEN

Panel 1: Darkness and painful cold. Richard signals for the others to follow as he speaks with Rob Huey (who counts his cash).

> ### 1. ROB
> I can stash the plane until you come back. But if anybody asks, I'll tell them you landed without permission and I just turned on the landing lights so you wouldn't splatter yourself all over Barrow.

Panel 2: Richard waves the others (Everybody in parkas. Keri, drags her bags, It's obviously torture for the teen to help) to load the truck. Rob looks at him stunned.

> ### 2. RICHARD
> Tell them whatever you like. I'll back you up if we run into anyone in town.

> ### 3. RICHARD 2
> Everybody load up the Hummer!

PAGE FOURTEEN

Panel 1: Rob argues with the smug Richard (Dressed in what looks like the complete Eddy Bauer winter collection) as the others (Nat, Scott, Chris, Tina, Keri) listen and load the hummer in the harsh cold.

ROB

> Town?
> (connected)
> You said you weren't going into town? Barrow is in lockdown. You show up at the gates and they'll know I let you land!

> ### 2. RICHARD
> And _THAT_ my friend is where we tell your lie and cover your ass.

anel 2: Rob Huey grips his cash as Richard opens the
river's side door. The Hummer is now packed and ready to
oll.

3. CAPTION
All Rob Huey can do is stand there with
a fistful of cash and wonder if it's
worth it.

anel 3: Rob shoves the cash in his parka, his hand coming
ack with a hand-cannon as his widened eyes dart around...

4. CAPTION
Even he knows deep down if these
jackasses go anywhere **but** Barrow,
they'll probably wind up dead.

anel 4: ...and suddenly Rob realizes he's alone, outside
he barbed UV light protected, Barrow.

5. CAPTION
If the cold didn't get them...

anel 5
ichard.

6. RICHARD
Not that I want to give that whelp at
the airport any added help, but I don't
care if we go into Barrow or not. It's
too well-protected. If we're going to
find any real action it's going to be
outside the fences.

anel 6
elly.

7. KELLY
But you promised! Keri and I want to
photograph Eben Olemaun's grave and the
remains of Ikos Diner.

anel 7
eri.

8. KERI
I don't want to take pictures of

anything. I don't even want to be here.

Panel 8
Kelly again, smiling.

9. KELLY
And the power station where Bill Lambert was beheaded!

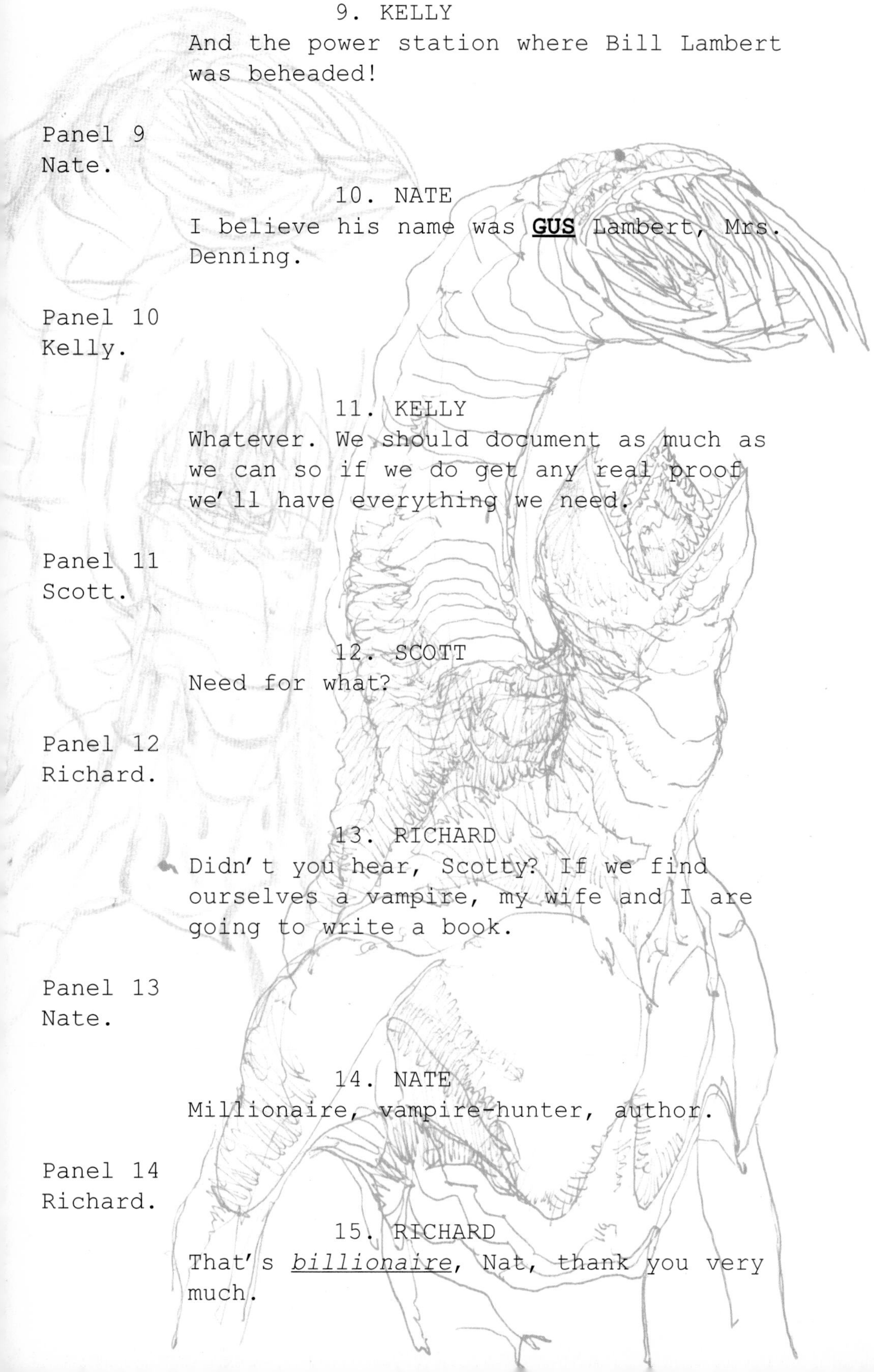

Panel 9
Nate.

10. NATE
I believe his name was **<u>GUS</u>** Lambert, Mrs. Denning.

Panel 10
Kelly.

11. KELLY
Whatever. We should document as much as we can so if we do get any real proof we'll have everything we need.

Panel 11
Scott.

12. SCOTT
Need for what?

Panel 12
Richard.

13. RICHARD
Didn't you hear, Scotty? If we find ourselves a vampire, my wife and I are going to write a book.

Panel 13
Nate.

14. NATE
Millionaire, vampire-hunter, author.

Panel 14
Richard.

15. RICHARD
That's <u>*billionaire*</u>, Nat, thank you very much.

PAGE FIFTEEN

Splash. The Hummer driving through the snow. Inset: In the back Keri sticks in her ipod earphones and shrinks down into her parka. She hates her parents SO much.

PAGES SIXTEEN & SEVENTEEN

DESCRIPTION: Barrow proper. The front gates look more like a checkpoint in Baghdad than the entrance to a small Alaskan town. There are armed guards, razor wire and a tower with a UV spotlight.

DESCRIPTION: As the Hummer approaches the gate GUARD ONE holds up his hand and blocks the path standing in the headlights of the massive vehicle.

DESCRIPTION: Guard One, a burly bearded man in a green parka wearing goggles and holding an assault rifle stands outside Richard's (now) rolled down window.

> 1. GUARD
> What's your business here?

Panel 2

DESCRIPTION: The Guards looks leery. Silent beat panel.

DESCRIPTION: And the Guard speaks as the other guards raise their rifles and aim at the Hummer.

> 2. RICHARD
> Just visiting.

> 3. GUARD
> This ain't exactly tourist season.

> 4. RICHARD
> Just want to see the sights and we'll be
> on our way.

> 5. GUARD
> You wanna come into Barrow, you gotta
> show us some identification...

DESCRIPTION: (Super-tight close-up?)

6. GUARD

...and your _TEETH_.

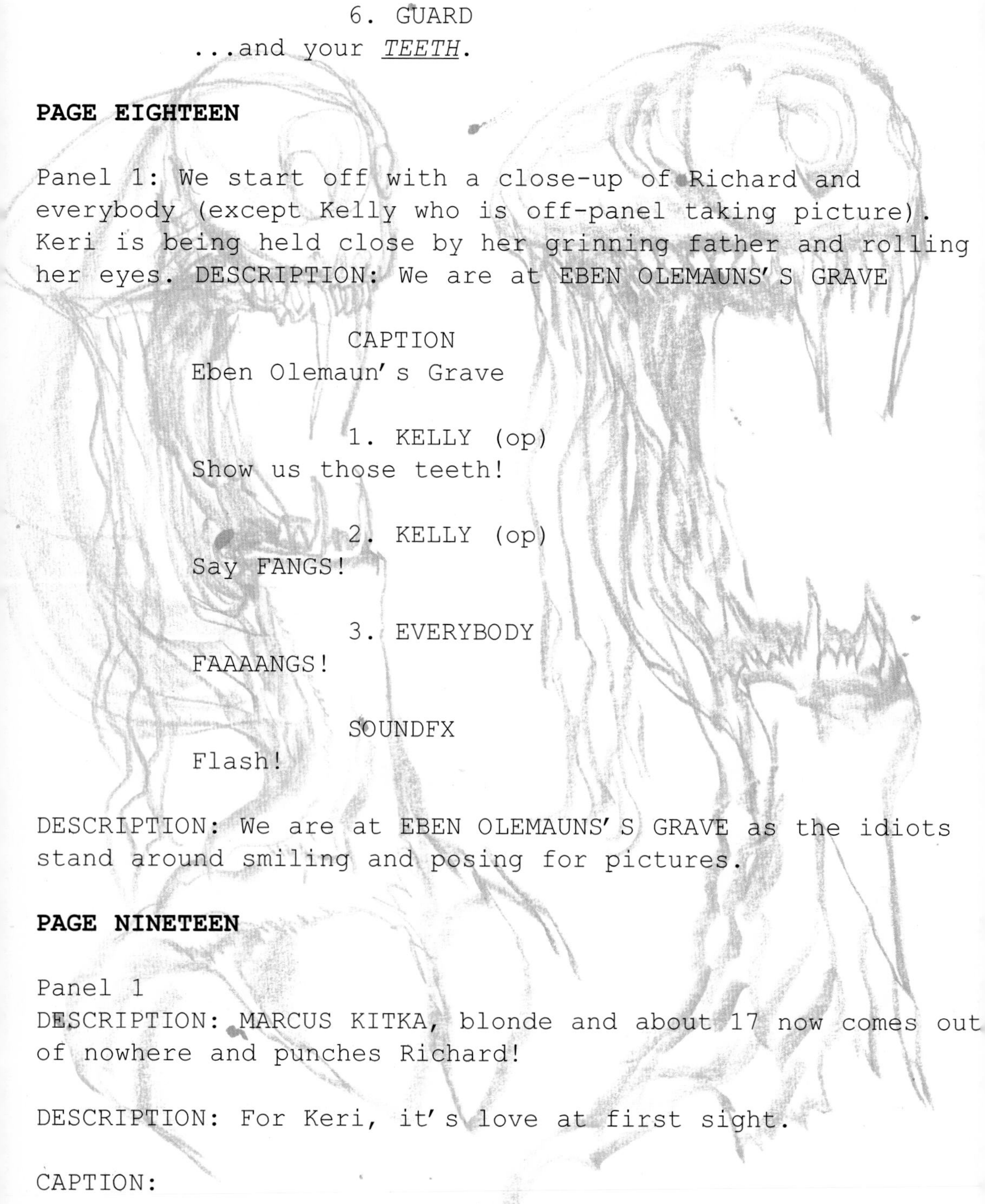

PAGE EIGHTEEN

Panel 1: We start off with a close-up of Richard and everybody (except Kelly who is off-panel taking picture). Keri is being held close by her grinning father and rolling her eyes. DESCRIPTION: We are at EBEN OLEMAUNS'S GRAVE

CAPTION

Eben Olemaun's Grave

1. KELLY (op)

Show us those teeth!

2. KELLY (op)

Say FANGS!

3. EVERYBODY

FAAAANGS!

SOUNDFX

Flash!

DESCRIPTION: We are at EBEN OLEMAUNS'S GRAVE as the idiots stand around smiling and posing for pictures.

PAGE NINETEEN

Panel 1

DESCRIPTION: MARCUS KITKA, blonde and about 17 now comes out of nowhere and punches Richard!

DESCRIPTION: For Keri, it's love at first sight.

CAPTION:

Marcus Kitka, 17. Barrow survivor.

DESCRIPTION: JOHN IKOS, the old trapper from 30 Days of Night: Return to Barrow, arrives in time to pull Marcus back and tell the folks they better have UV lights.

2. RICHARD

Yeah, we read the book. Don't worry, old man, we can handle

ourselves.

3. IKOS
For your families' sake, I
hope you're right.

4. CAPTION:
John Ikos. Considerably older than 17.
Barrow survivor.

PAGE TWENTY to end...

DESCRIPTION: The close of this issue is John Ikos and Marcus watching Richard Denning, Keri Denning and the rest of the adventurers getting back into the Hummer and heading out onto the tundra.

DESCRIPTION: They are headed right towards the mountains where the vampires were killed earlier.

DESCRIPTION: They don't even notice when the tank tread crushes a vampire's jawbone.

Issue closes on John Ikos speaking...

1. IKOS
Poor stupid bastards. I **almost** feel
sorry for them.

DESCRIPTION: And nobody, not even Ikos, is aware of the INHUMAN EYES that watch from the dark.

CAPTION:

To be continued...

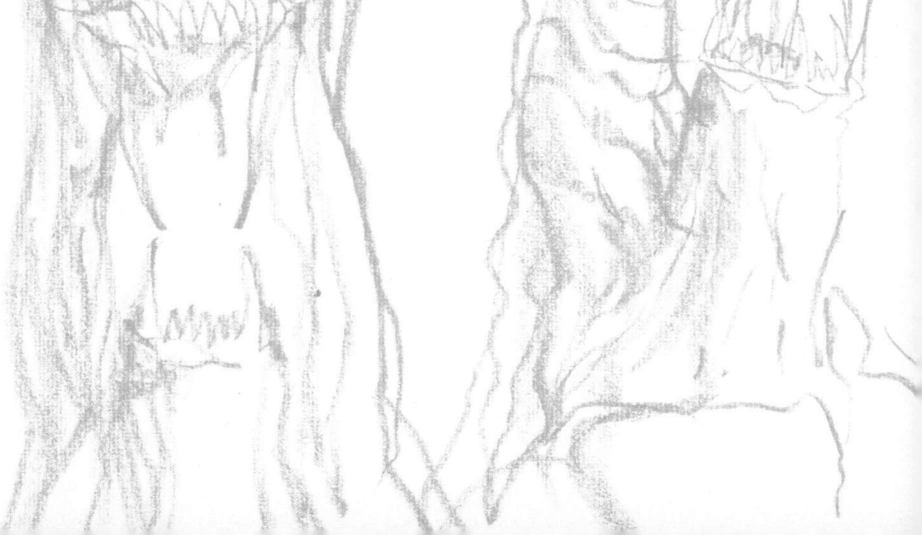

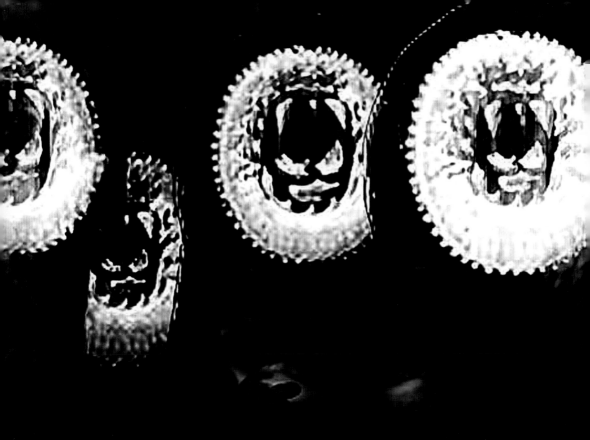

preliminary designs
bill sienkiewicz

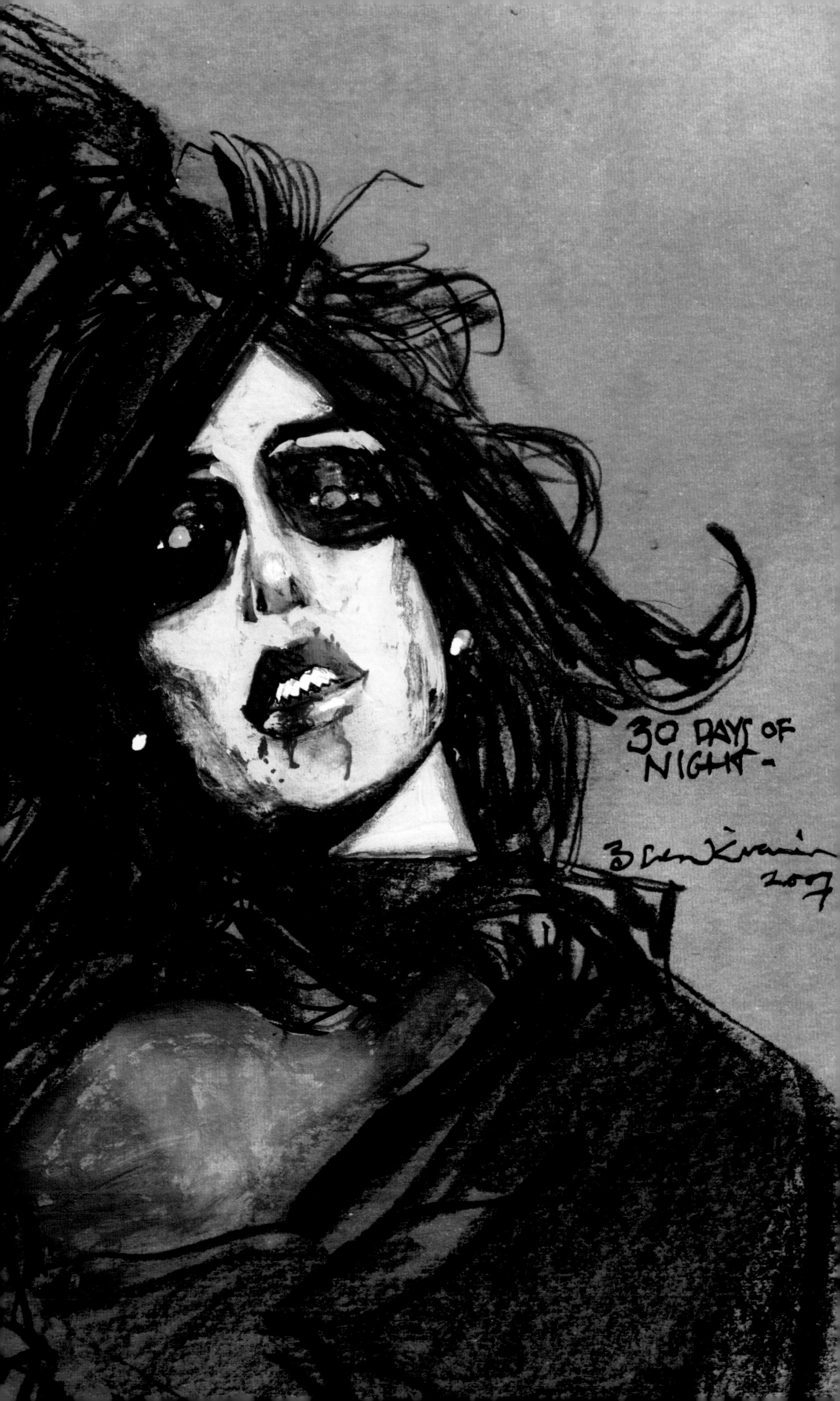
30 DAYS OF
NIGHT -

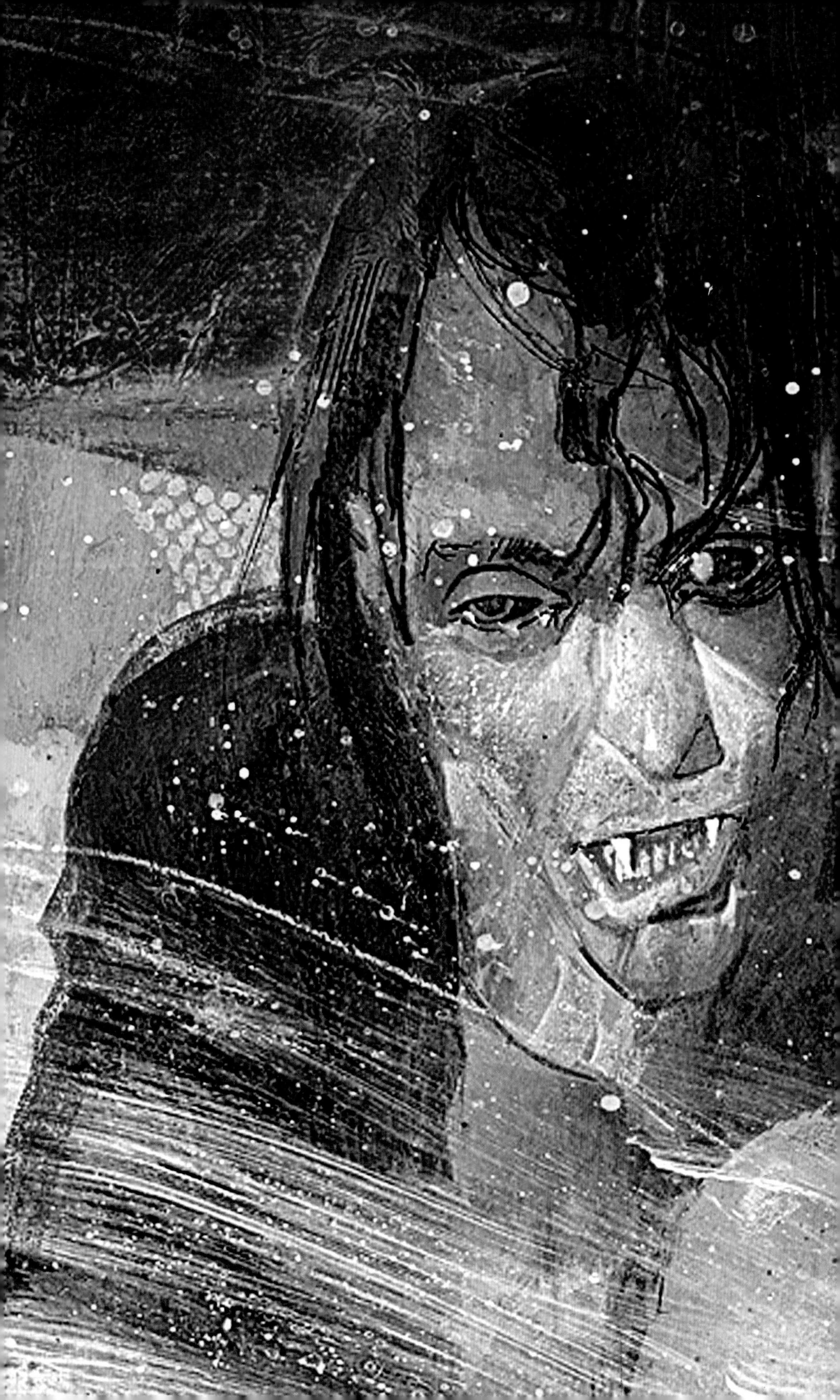

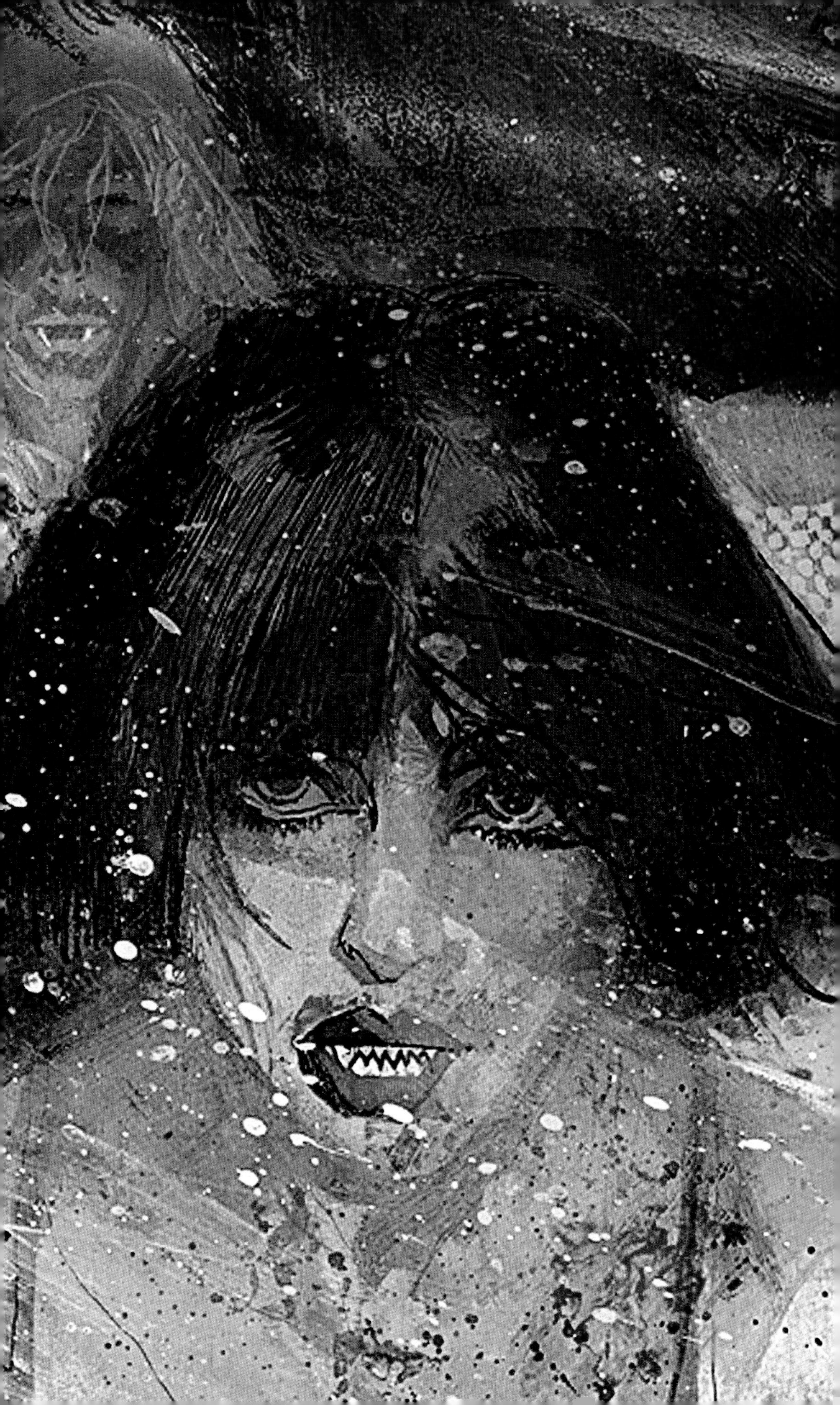

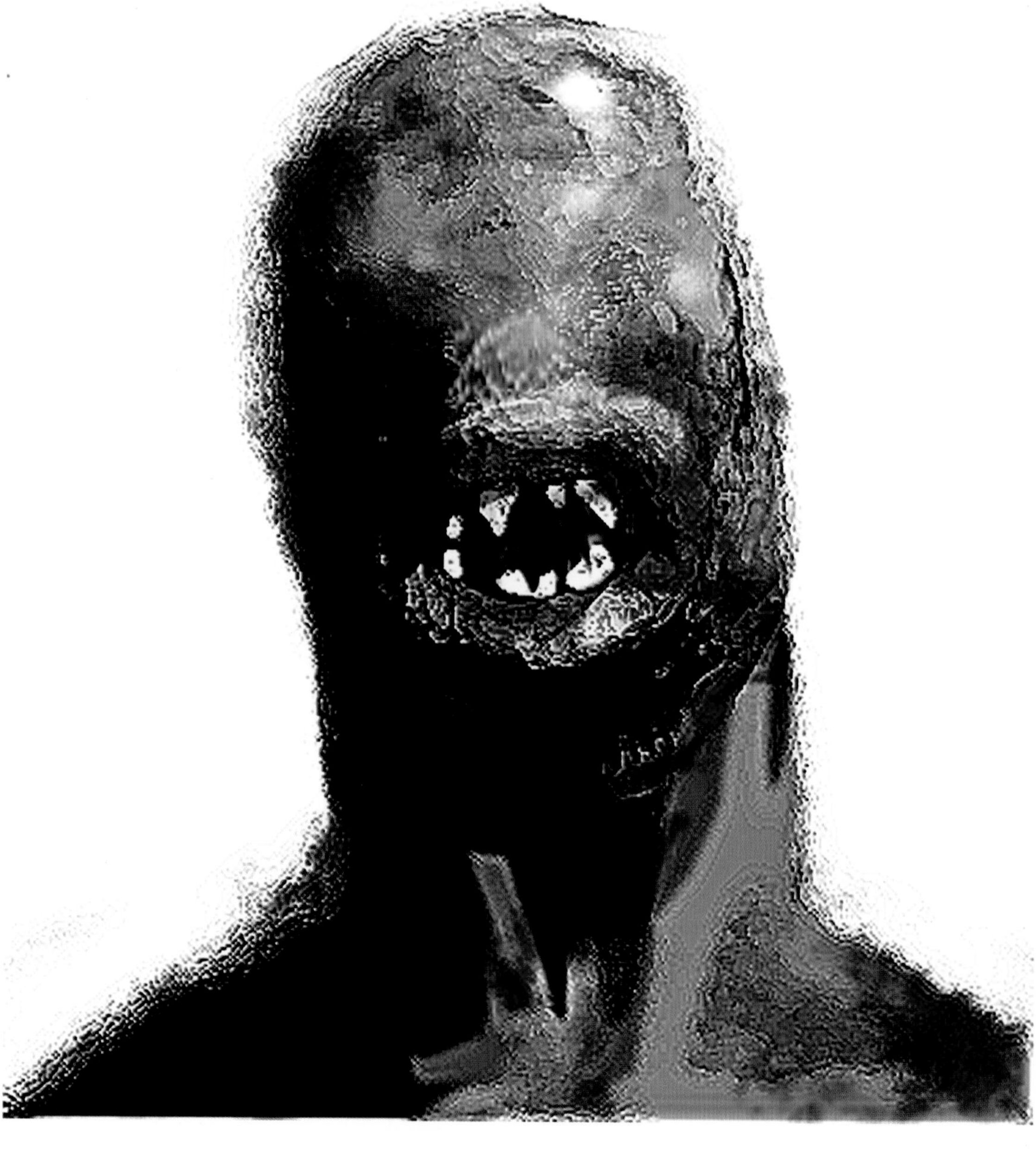

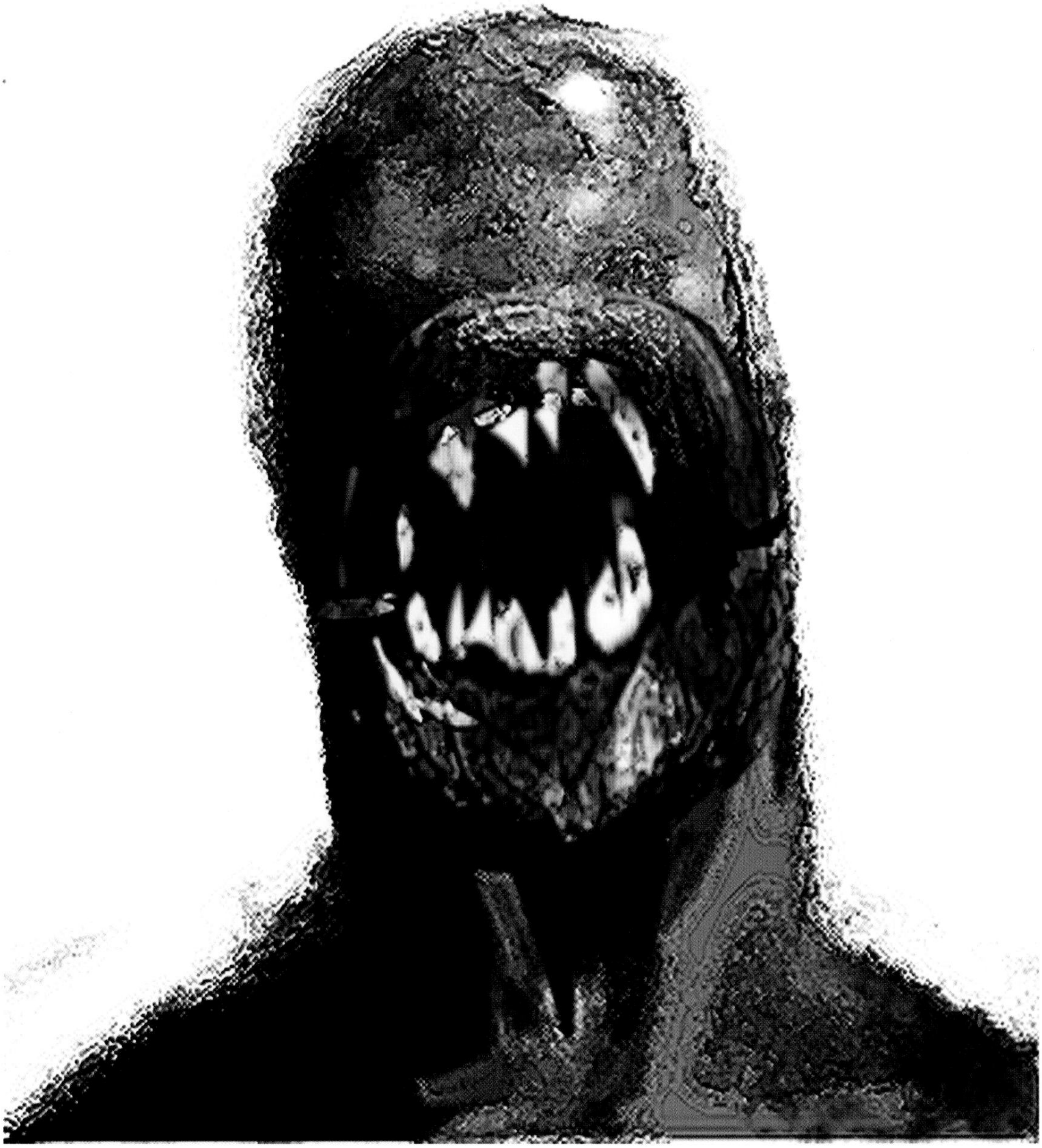

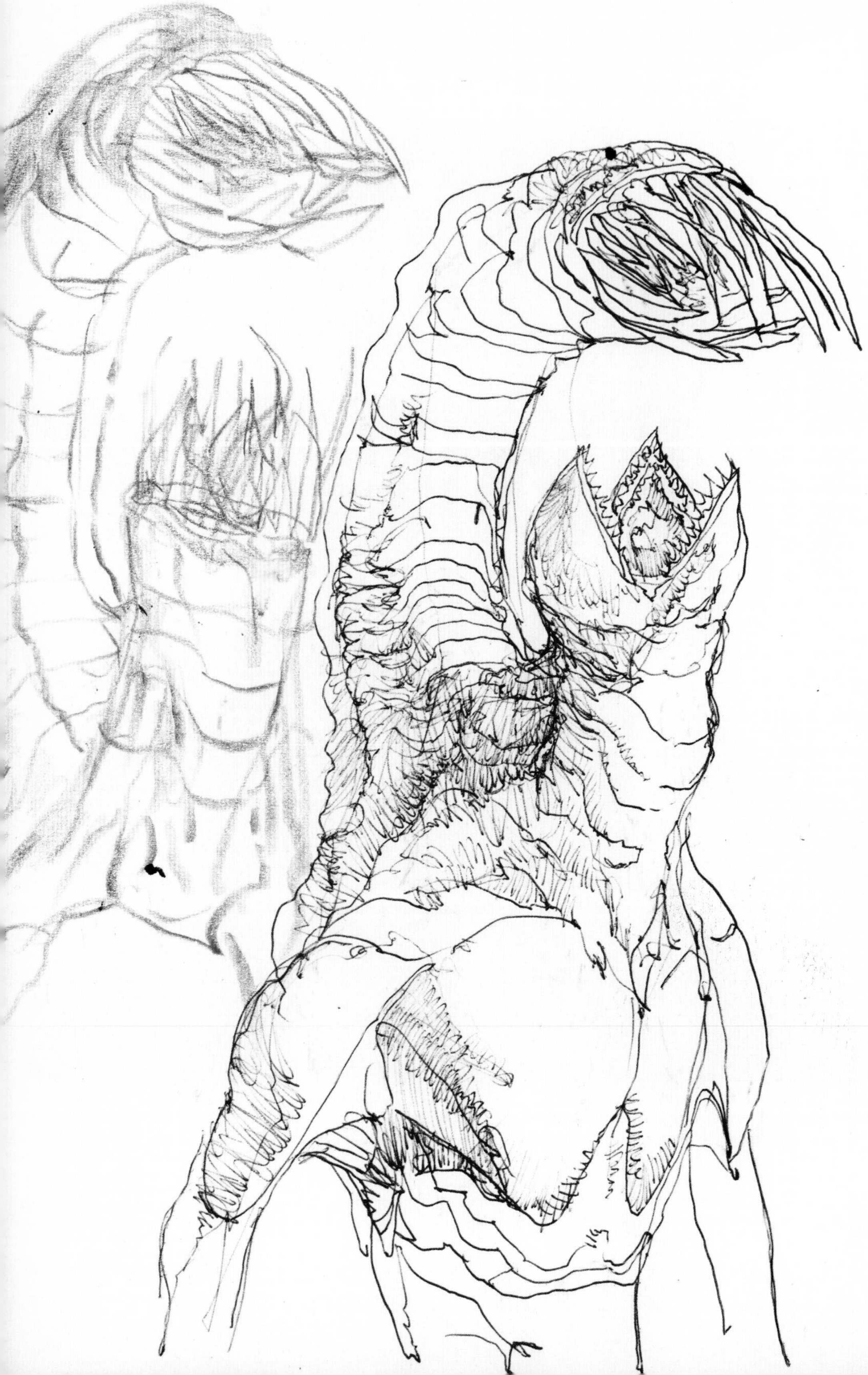

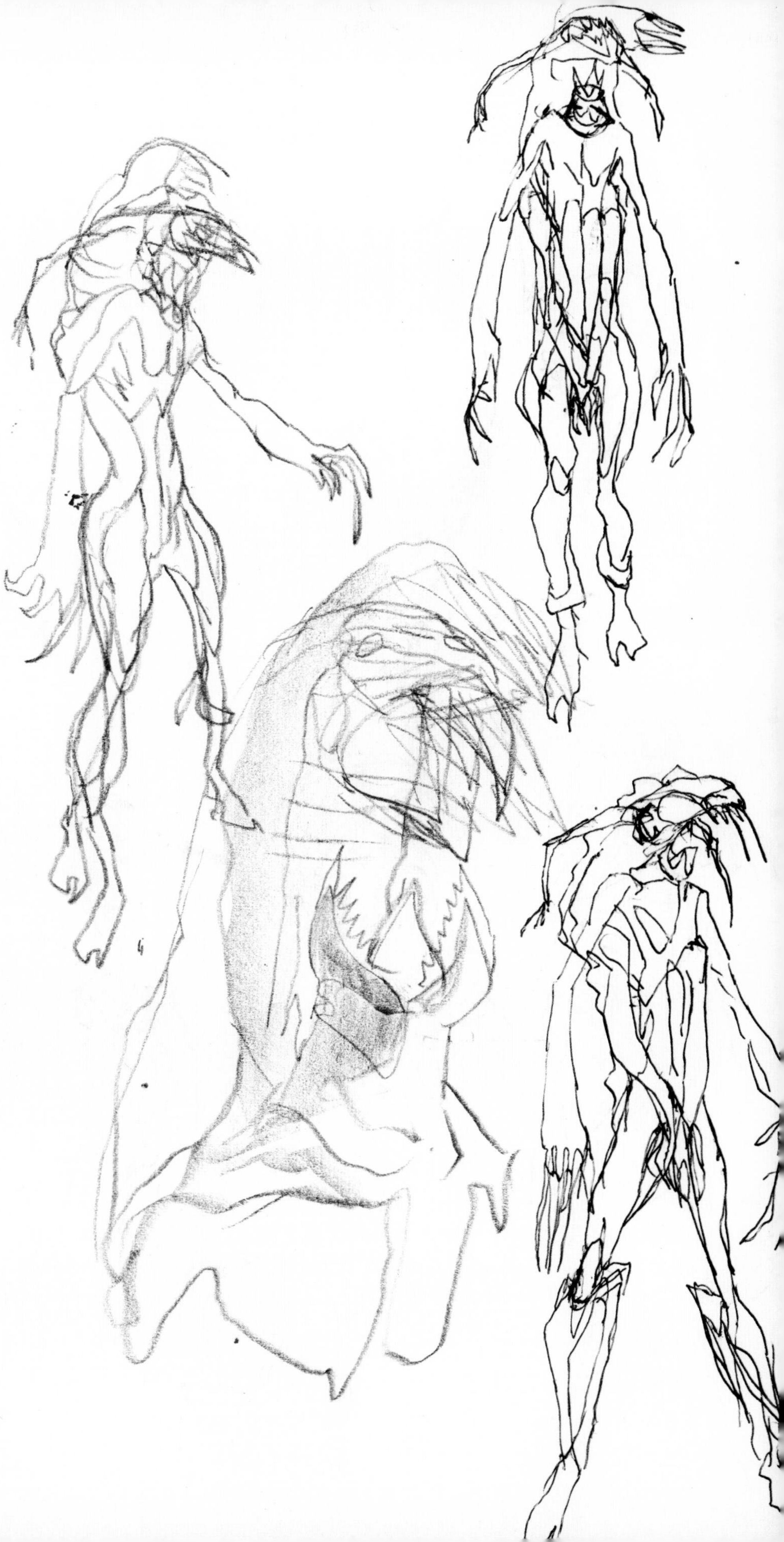

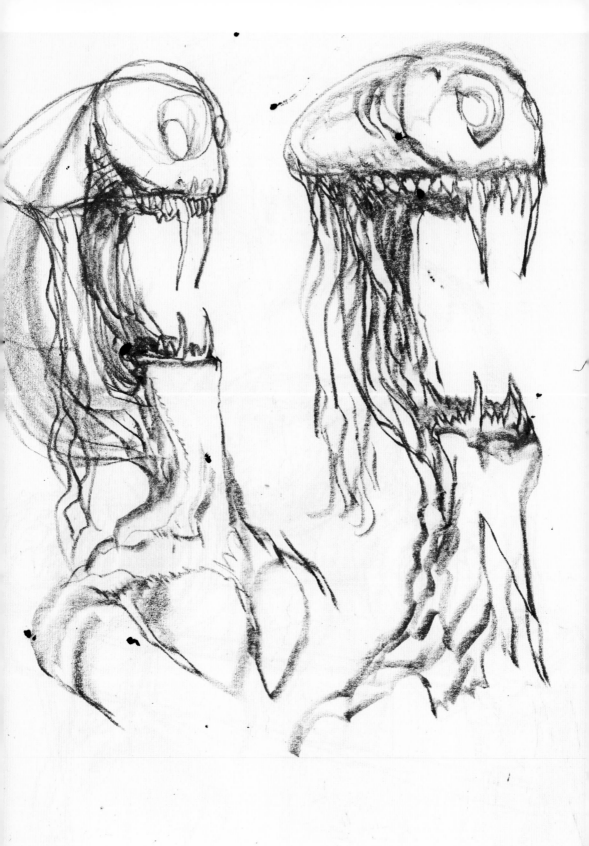

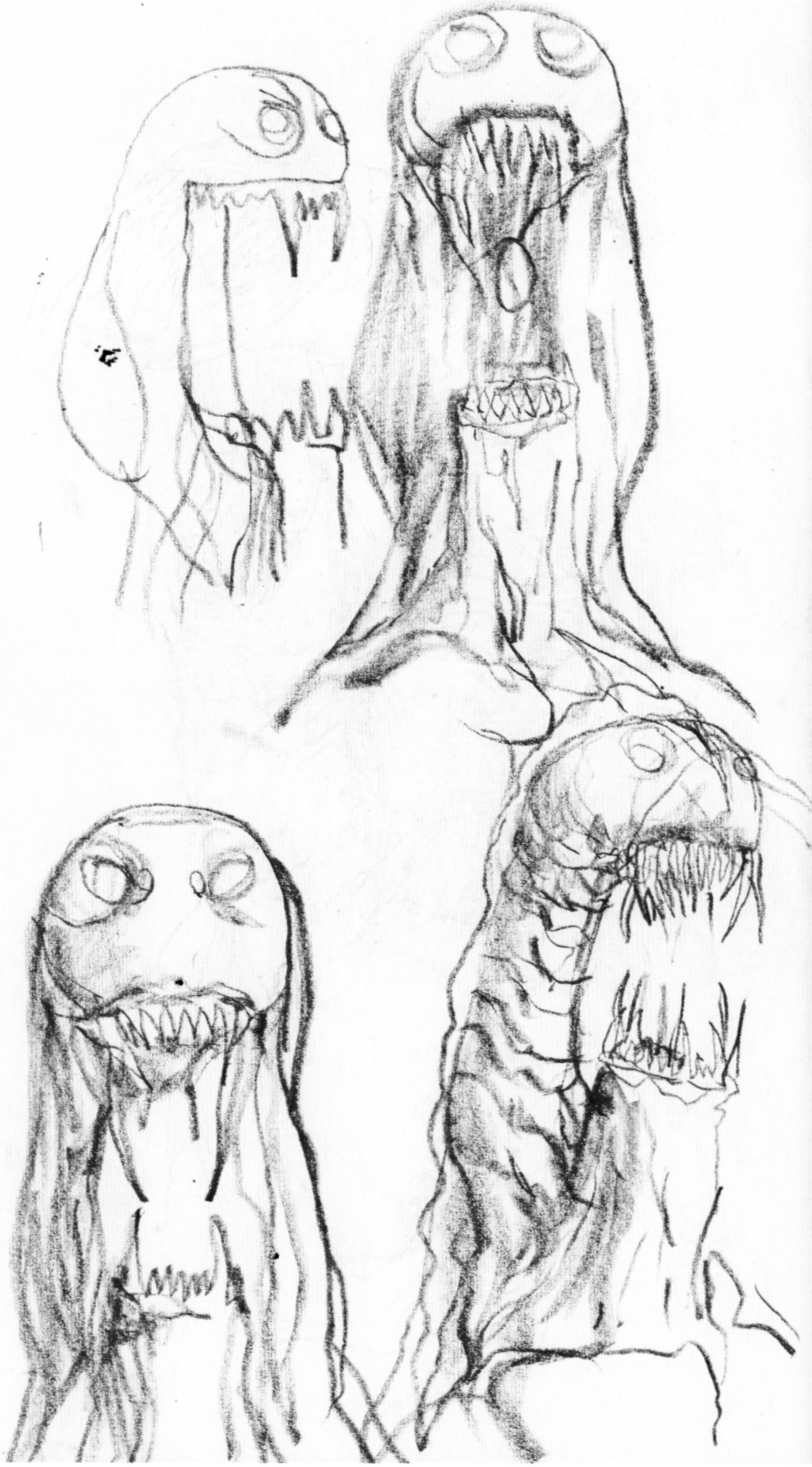

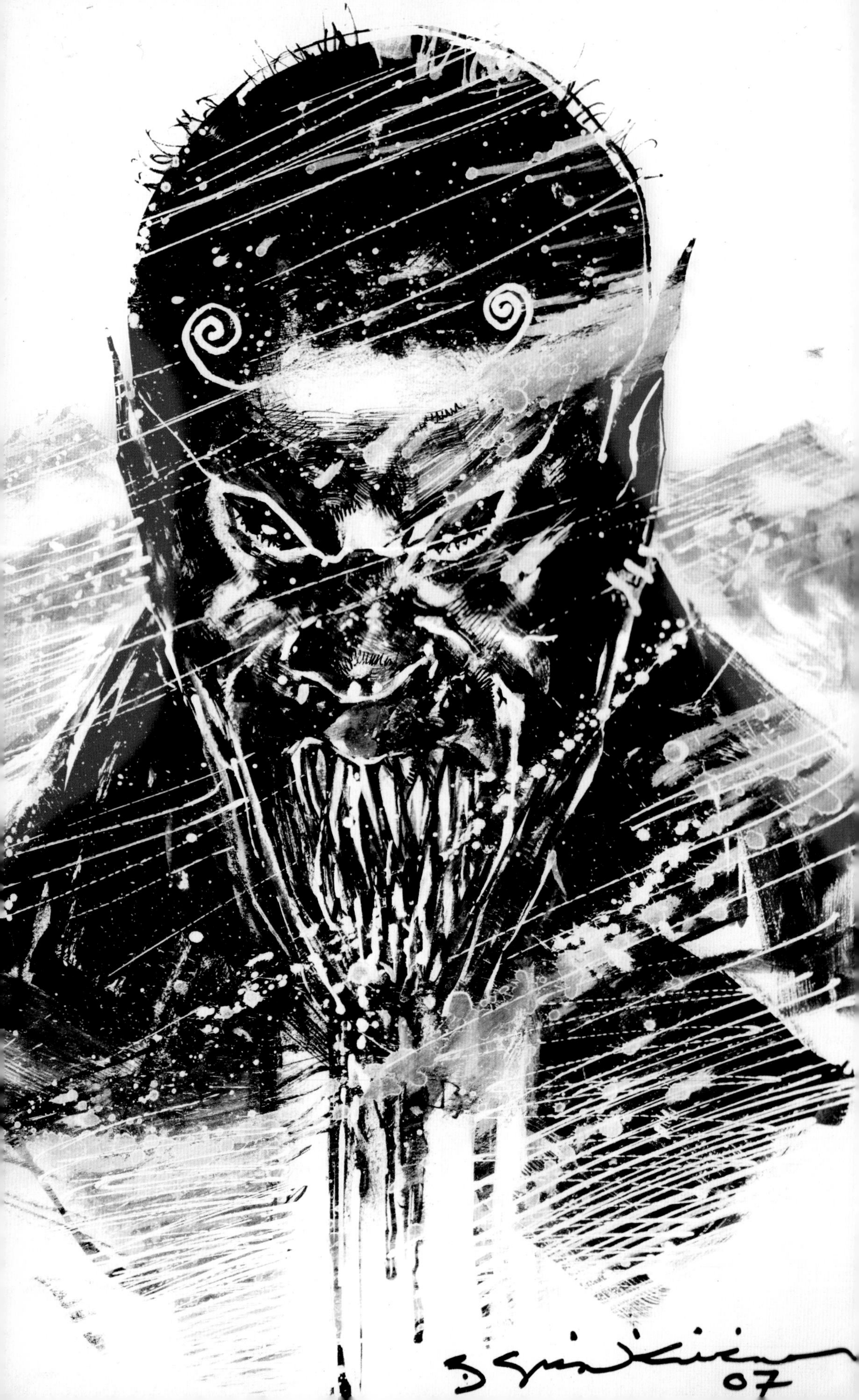
07